1967

Th.

CROSSCURRENTS *Modern Critiques*

CROSSCURRENTS *Modern Critiques*
Harry T. Moore, *General Editor*

Harry T. Moore

Twentieth-Century
French Literature
SINCE WORLD WAR II

Carbondale and Edwardsville

SOUTHERN ILLINOIS UNIVERSITY PRESS

London and Amsterdam

FEFFER AND SIMONS, INC.

To Caresse Crosby

CONTENTS

INTRODUCTION

THIS IS THE SECOND of two volumes dealing with the French literature of the twentieth century. The first one carried the subject from the beginning of the century, and the Dreyfus case, up through the Second World War; the present one takes it beyond that war and into the 1960's.

This work has been divided into two volumes simply because of length. They were originally planned as a unit, part of a study not merely of French but of all contemporary European literature. Since the French material has been finished first, it will be published first. The introduction to this volume repeats some of the points made in the introduction to its predecessor, though it adds a few too.

The book deals with three principal genres: poetry, fiction, and drama. It gives special attention to the avant garde, the innovators, but also grants a good deal of space to various traditional authors. Indeed, one long section of the present volume deals with novelists of the traditionalist stamp; I couldn't include all of them, and in many cases could mention only a limited number of works by certain authors. The chapter is not strictly up to date, but since the original intention of this book was to bring the material only up to 1960, I regard it as a bit of extra dividend if this volume can provide, in several cases, mention of a few later works. The absolute terminal date is the day late in 1965 on which this volume went to the printers'. In any event, that section on recent traditional novelists is the most tentative of all, since some of the authors it deals with may not survive, though now is really too early to determine. I simply took some of the best of the traditional novelists and wrote about them. I feel more certain about authors dealt with in other parts of this volume, particularly the members of the existential, antiliterature, and absurdity groups.

It should be stressed here that this book, like its predecessor, is introductory. The method is historical and expository. If seasoned readers of French literature find that my putting all this material together has made some new perspectives possible, I'll be pleased. But it must be said again that the work is introductory. Of course no secondary type of book can convey the deep excitement of contemporary French literature, which itself deserves reading. I can only hope that the present effort will bring new readers to that literature. There are good translations, but preferably the books should be explored in the original. Many of us have a few French courses tucked away in our past. Anyhow, this book and its predecessor are meant to be not only guides but inducements. As for the material translated in these pages, virtually all of it is my own, as all the poems are; none of the translations have any pretensions beyond what is known as "free" rendering.

Experienced readers of French literature may feel that some of their favorites are slighted in these pages or omitted altogether. Such a consequence is inevitable in books of this kind: every reader is of course his own historian and critic. I can only hope that I have neglected no major figure and have given a fair hearing to the writers usually thought of as minor.

Now for a few technical points to explain certain usages. The titles of the books under consideration present a problem, particularly because many of them appear in English with quite different names; that is, not in literal translation. Hence, with the first mention of each book I have given the French title, plus an English rendition as accurate as possible, adding the translated title—if I could locate it—when this differs from the literal. And for the sake of compactness each first reference to a book contains its publication date; with plays, the year of first production.

As an example, we have in the text "Pierre-Henri Simon's *Portrait d'un officier* (1958; *Portrait of an Officer*, also translated as *An End to Glory*)." In England, the book appeared as *Portrait of an Officer*, but in the United States as *An End to Glory*. I couldn't discuss *An End to Glory* without making clear which of Simon's books I was referring to, since the title *An End to Glory* doesn't suggest the French original.

In all cases I have included titles in the text itself, at the point at which the authors of the books in question are being discussed. Admittedly, this now and then crowds the text with titles, particularly when it lists a number of books by one author, as in the treatment of George Duhamel's *The Pasquier Chronicles*. Putting all these data into a bibliography at the end would impose a burden on the reader by making him turn to the back of the book whenever he wanted full information. Similarly, placing the material at the bottom of each page concerned would make many pages simply chaotic, and the reader would still have to break his reading to look down and find what he wanted to know. Consequently, I have put everything into the text; if the reader wants to skip over the details of a cluster of titles, his eyes can simply reach beyond and continue their progress. This is a matter of method, and it seems the least painful one.

I have provided biographical information, some of it necessarily brief, though fairly full where major authors are concerned, particularly writers whose work bears a close relation to their lives. The text also attempts to describe and define various literary movements which have characterized French literature in this century. I have generally used French spellings, such as symbolisme, surréalisme, and existentialisme, though in the main have avoided italics for French words and phrases because the text already contains so much italicized material in the way of titles.

The preceding volume, in discussing the literature of the Second World War—a literature that came out of the conditions that created that war—dealt with the earlier phases of existentialisme and of such authors as Jean-Paul Sartre and Albert Camus, whose later work is taken up here. Once again, there is a close connection between the two books.

In closing, I should like to acknowledge benefits derived from several critical histories of French literature and studies of individual authors. In English, these include books by Germaine Brée, Victor Brombert, John Cruikshank, Wallace Fowlie, W. H. Frohock, Thomas Hanna, Rayner Heppenstall, Laurent Le Sage, and Henri Peyre, among others; in French, by Pierre de Boisdeffre, Pierre Brodin, Gaëtan Picon, and Bernard Pingaud, among others. Various friends whom I shall not enumerate here have also helped, and I hope they will accept this general statement of thanks. I must mention a special indebtedness to Alan Cohn, Humanities Librarian at Southern Illinois University, who is not, however, to be held responsible for any mistakes which may occur in these pages. And I am exceedingly grateful for the assistance given by the John Simon Guggenheim Memorial Foundation; parts of this project, some not yet completed, were begun while I held a Guggenheim Fellowship that helped me to carry on various phases of these studies in Europe.

HARRY T. MOORE

Southern Illinois University
October 12, 1965

Twentieth-Century French Literature
SINCE WORLD WAR II

A GOOD DEAL of French postwar poetry has been written by prewar and wartime poets such as Francis Ponge and Henri Michaux, both born in 1899. Ponge's first important publication was in 1942, although as early as 1926 he brought out the volume *Douze Petits Écrits* (*Twelve Little Writings*). His 1942 book, *Le Parti pris des choses* (*The Set Purpose of Things*), in its very title accented Ponge's constant preoccupation with the thing, the object. Michaux also began publishing in the 1920's, but didn't attain full recognition until later. One of the boosts to Michaux's career came when the Vichy authorities, through the new Fascist "Legion," hinted to André Gide in 1941 that it would be better if he didn't give a proposed lecture on Michaux in Nice; Gide subsequently published the undelivered lecture as *Découvrons Henri Michaux* (1941; *Let us Discover Henri Michaux*), and this greatly increased the poet's reputation.

Francis Ponge was born in Montpellier. He chiefly writes prose poems of the most concrete kind: to bread, a cigarette, an oyster, fire, a butterfly, a tree trunk, water. Unlike most French poets since Baudelaire, Ponge is not concerned with the inner life; his verse anticipated the novels of the *école du regard* of Robbe-Grillet and others. The almost ferocious intensity with which Ponge looks at, into, and through an object seems almost as if he, instead of Guy de Maupassant, were the pupil of Gustave Flaubert, who once told his disciple that, in order to describe a fire or a tree, it was necessary to remain before such objects until they no longer looked like any other fire or tree; a grocer in his doorway, a concierge puffing away at his pipe, a horse at a cabstand, all have a distinct individuality which exactly the right word can properly express—the precise verb can make it move, the unique adjective can qualify it. In describing a cigarette, for example, Ponge first establishes the setting, with the mist of smoke in opposition to the dry body of the cigarette; then he describes the cigarette "herself," with her fire and perfume and her bits of ash that fall in a calculable rhythm as the cigarette lies in her usually horizontal position; then there is the "passion" of the cigarette as it is consumed. The description has not only the Flaubertian exactness, but the poem also seems to invest the cigarette with a symbolic meaning, making it virtually a representation of the Heraclitean idea of fire as essential universal motion.

In "l'Huître" ("The Oyster"), Ponge finds this brilliantly whitish object "a stubbornly closed world." But one opens it with a knife that is curved and hardly honest. Inside, after delivering some blows that give the shell a kind of halo, one finds a whole world for eating and drinking, with nothing less than a firmament, and heavens above and beneath making a pool, really "a sack slimy and green which flows back and forth in odor and sight, fringed with blackish lace at its borders." And once in a great while, a pearl will be found in there. The poem seems to find all creation in this single mollusc, with the possibility of rare beauty.

Many of Ponge's poems which have appeared in journals were uncollected until 1962. Before that, he occasionally brought out a volume, such as *Dix Courts sur la méthode* (1946; *Ten Briefs on Method*) and *Proêmes* (1948; *Introductions*). Ponge has published his exercise books that show how he works to make his poems; these notebooks, including "Le Carnet du bois de pins" ("The Notebook of the Pinewood"), appear in *La Rage de l'expression* (1952; *The Fury of Expression*). In 1954,

Ponge's *Nouvelle Revue française* poem, "Le Soleil placé
en abîme" ("The Sun Placed in an Abyss"), brought
together this poet's exactness of observation with a
philosophical vision. The summary of Ponge's work is in
the three-volume *Le Grand Recueil* (1962; *The Great
Collection*): 1. *Lyres*, 2. *Méthodes*, 3. *Pièces*. This miscel-
lany shows Ponge at his most effective in his concentration upon phenomena. He is one of the principal
literary ancestors of the nouveau roman (new novel).

Belgian-born Henri Michaux is, like Ponge, for the
most part a writer of prose poems, but where Ponge looks
outward, Michaux looks inward. Indeed, he called a large
selection of his writings in 1944 *l'Espace de dedans* (*The
Space Within*, creatively translated by Richard Ellmann).
Not that Michaux doesn't write of the outer world, for
many of his poems reflect his early experiences as a sailor
who traveled to many exotic places, from the Amazon
(see *Ecuador*, 1929) to the Orient (see *Un Barbare on
Asie*, 1932; *A Barbarian in Asia*). Yet he projects everything as within a dream; Gide said that Michaux recalled
Nietzsche's statement, "Only in our dreams are we utterly
sincere." Gide added that Michaux made one intuitively
feel the strangeness of the natural and the naturalness of
the strange.

Michaux, who avoids having his picture taken because
people might recognize him in the métro, had a shy childhood; it was, he has written, a time when he clenched his
teeth against life. And his poems give little indication that
he has found peace of nerves. French by choice, Michaux
lives in Paris where, besides writing poetry, he paints and
regularly exhibits his work (gouaches and water colors),
though generally remaining aloof from artistic cliques and
the literary life. Besides *The Space Within*, which collected most of Michaux's earlier work from *Que Je fus*
(1927; *Who I Was*) through his writings of the early
1940's, some of his subsequent books include: *Épreuves,
Exorcismes* (1945; *Ordeals and Exorcisms*), *Ici, Podema*
(1946; *Here, Podema*), *Passages* (1950), *Face aux Verrous*
(1954; *Face the Bolts*), *Misérable Miracle* (1955), *l'Infini*

turbulent (1957; *Turbulent Infinity*), *Paix dans les brisements* (1959; *Peace in Trouble*), and *Connaissance par les gouffres* (1961; *Knowledge from the Gulf*). In *Nous deux encore* (1948; *We Two Together*), Michaux writes of his relationship with his wife, who was killed in an accident in 1948.

One of the typical projections of Michaux's experience is his book *Plume* (1937), in which he takes a kind of everyman who is yet a special man—something like Franz Kafka's character called K. in *The Trial*—and shows how fragile and helpless he is in the grip of daily events. In one of the *Plume* poems, for example (which appeared first in an early volume, *Un Certain Plume—A Certain Plume*— in 1931), we find Plume reaching his hands out of bed and, to his surprise, not touching the wall. He tells himself the ants must have eaten it, and he sinks back into sleep. But his wife shakes him and tells him that, while he has slept, someone has stolen the house: "And indeed, unbroken sky stretched above them on every side." Plume thinks to himself, "Bah, the thing's done." But soon he hears and sees a train rushing at them. Thinking, "it will certainly get there before we do," Plume goes to sleep again. When cold wakes him up, he finds himself drenched in blood, with fragments of his wife lying next to him. Blood is unpleasant, he reflects, and if the train could have avoided them, he would have been pleased. But it has gone by, so he returns to sleep. Then a judge is asking him how it happens that Plume didn't help his wife or even notice that she was being cut into eight pieces: "There's the mystery," the judge concludes. "The entire case is in that." Plume feels that he can be of no help in this and drops off to sleep again. Then a voice tells him the execution will take place the next day and asks him whether he, the accused, has anything to add. Plume replies, "Excuse me. I haven't been following this case." And he goes back to sleep.

One of France's most popular poets, whose verses are often sung in nightclubs, Jacques Prévert was born in 1900. Influenced originally by surréalisme, later by Marxism, Prévert first attracted attention with the comic fantasy, *Tentative de description d'un dîner de têtes à Paris-France* (1931; *Attempt at a Description of a Dinner of Disguised Guests in Paris, France*). Some of Prévert's other books include: *Paroles* (1946; *Words*), *Spectacles* (1951), and *La Pluie et le beau temps* (1955: *Rain and Good Weather*). Usually satirical, Prévert often takes the pomp of office for his target; he uses every twist of language, filling his work with puns and slang. But he can describe with tenderness an unknown girl seen in the rain, as in "Barbara," which begins:

> *Remember, Barbara,*
> *It rained without ceasing over Brest that day*
> *And you walked smiling*
> *Blooming delighted dripping*
> *Under the rain*

as the poet passed her in the rue de Siam, learning her name when a man sheltered under a porch called it out, and she ran to him; she was dripping and delighted and blooming as she threw herself into his arms. The poet over the distance of time tells Barbara not to forget that wise and happy rain on her happy face and on that happy town. Then the mood changes; how vicious war is:

> *What has become of you now*
> *Beneath this rain of iron*
> *Of fire of steel of blood*
> *And he who held you in his arms*
> *Lovingly*
> *Is he dead missing or still alive*
> *Oh Barbara*
> *It rains without ceasing over Brest*
> *As it rained before. . . .*

but it is different, and everything is ruined in this awful, desolate rain of grief, which is not even the storm of rain and steel and blood; the clouds simply die like dogs that disappear in the waters beside Brest and go far away to rot, "Far very far from Brest / Of which nothing remains."

Raymond Queneau, the novelist, has in common with

Prévert the fact that his poems are often sung in cafés. Some of his volumes of verse beginning with his autobiographical narrative in poetry, *Chêne et chien* (1937; *Oak and Dog*), include *Les Ziaux* (1943), *Petite Cosmogonie portative* (1950; *Little Portable World-Philosophy*), *Si Tu t'imagines* (1952; *If You Imagine*), and *Cent Mille Milliards de Poèmes* (1961; *Hundred Thousand Billion Poems*). As in his prose works, Queneau in his poetry plays with language, often chewing it up into what he calls the new or third French language: "Moi, je suis de Paris" becomes "Moua chsui dpari," and the familiar "n'est-ce pas" becomes "spa." This kind of word play is noticeable in the title poem of *If You Imagine*, in which the repeated "xa va" undoubtedly makes fun of "ça va," and "la saison des za" possibly means "la saison des saisons" ("the season of seasons"). The poem itself, made famous in the cafés by Juliette Greco in an expert gamine rendering of gaminerie, using the vulgar reflexive se gourer (to be wrong):

> *If you imagine*
> *if you imagine*
> *little girl little girl*
> *if you imagine*
> *that it's going that it's going that*
> *it's going to last forever*
> *the season of s'sons*
> *the season of s'sons*
> *the season of loves—*

if she imagines all these things, she's got it wrong.

René Char, born in 1907, was one of the leaders of the maquis in the résistance. In his youth he was briefly a member of the surréaliste group, which probably helped pique his imagination and extended the range of his word power, but he has remained essentially a hermetic poet, a poet of magic and philosophy, frequently invoking as well as evoking Heraclitus and often writing in an aphoristic manner. Char has spent most of his life in his native Provence, and his work is full of the Mediterranean atmosphere, the almond trees, mimosas, fig trees, olive trees, and the vineyards wandering over the low hills. A poet of the soil, Char is the opponent of mechanization and of cities. He has written with pastoral sagacity in a tense music, and has been called one of the great poets of Provence and of all modern France.

The poems of *Le Marteau sons maître* (1934; *The Masterless Hammer*) were surréaliste, but they marked his farewell to that mode. Char developed a sense of engagement when he brooded over the fate of the children who were victims of the Spanish Civil War, and he wrote poetry about modern social problems in *Placard pour un chemin des écoliers* (1937; *Poster for a School-boys' Road*). The sense of engagement continued in his wartime poems, *Seuls demeurent* (1945; *They Live Alone*) and *Feuillets d'Hypnos* (1946; *Leaves of Hyp-nos*). These books, little read now, were poems of force coming directly out of the experience of men fighting guerrilla war. The later Char, writing from Provence, appears in *Fureur et mystère* (1948; *Furor and Mystery*), which reproduced Hypnos' journal. Char in his verse maxims made it clear that he considers poetry the result of the conflict between furor and mystery, but that it also comes out of the interaction of many forces: "Between innocence and knowledge, love and nothingness, the poet daily increases his health."

Other volumes by Char include: *Le Poème pulvérisé* (1947; *The Pulverized Poem*), *Les Matinaux* (1950; *The Early Mornings*), *À une Sérénité crispée* (1951; *To a Tensed Serenity*), *Lettera amorosa* (1953), *Recherche de la base et du sommet* (1955; *Search of the Base and the Summit*), *Poèmes et prose choisis* (1957; *Selected Poems and Prose*), and *La Fausse Relève* (1959; *The False Relief*). He has, in his recent work, tended increasingly toward the prose poem, though much of his work is in free verse. One of the finest examples of the latter is from *The Pulverized Poem*, the one beginning, "Mon Amour à la robe de phrase bleue":

> *My love whose dress is a blue beacon*
> *I kiss the fever of your face*
> *where the light sleeps that enjoys itself in secret.*

I love and I weep. I am alive
And your heart is this Morning Star
of the victorious endurance that blushed before
breaking as under the battle of Constellations.

With you, may my flesh become the sail
which feels the wind repugnant.

Here the beloved woman is exalted: her very dress is a beacon of blue, the light enjoys her face, her heart is the morning star, and without her the elemental wind is disgusting to the lover, whose flesh is the sail to which the wind is repugnant. The antinomies, the clashing opposites of Heraclitus, show through this poem, which keeps its breathless quality to the last moment; in Heraclitean fashion, the writing of Char is always in the process of becoming.

André Frénaud, born in 1907, in *Les Rois Mages* (1943; *The Wise Kings*) expressed, in a kind of existential despair, the feelings of Frenchmen during the occupation. After the war he published *Les Paysans* (1947; *The Peasants*); his work is intellectually severe, but often lacking in music. Patrice de la Tour du Pin, born in 1911, writes chiefly of the Sologne country south of Paris, his native landscape. His *Quête de joie* (1933; *Quest of Joy*) attracted favorable attention. Wounded in the war and taken prisoner, he afterward brought out *Une Somme de poésie* (1947; A *Summary of Poetry*), six hundred pages of verse with some prose passages. *Le Second Jeu* (*The Second Game*) appeared in 1959. Classical in style, La Tour du Pin has created his own myths, largely hermetic, working them out against the background of the Sologne. Aimé Césaire is a Negro poet, born in 1912 in Martinique, who studied at the École normale in Paris. He later represented Martinique as a Communist deputy, but broke with his colleagues after the Budapest uprising was crushed by Soviet arms in 1956. Césaire has been one of the great exponents of what the French call négritude, the celebration of the condition of being a Negro and the demand for freedom from colonial and other bonds; in his more recent work, however, Césaire is less the poet of négritude than of all humanity. Césaire's volumes of poetry include *Les Armes miraculeuses* (1946; *The Miraculous Arms*), *Corps perdu* (1949; *Lost Body,* illustrated by Picasso), and *Ferrements* (1960; *Iron Shackles*), the last telling the story of the enslavement of his ancestors, brought to an end by their own protests. Césaire in his poems frequently uses rhythmic effects associated with Negroes, from the tam-tam of North Africa and the batouque of Brazil to the blues of Harlem. Another Martinique poet, Édouard Glissant (born 1928), whose volumes of verse include *Un Champ d'îles* (1953; *A Field of Islands*), *La Terre inquiète* (1956; *The Unquiet Earth*), and *Le Sel noir* (1960; *Black Salt*), is also the author of *La Lézarde* (1958; *The Crevice*), a novel which won the Prix Théophraste Renaudot. A poet who didn't live to fulfill his promise, Jean-Paul de Dadelson (1914–57), is represented chiefly in the rather fragmentary volume *Jonas* (1962). Dadelson didn't begin writing verses until he was thirty-eight; his work is mature, usually existential in outlook, and radiant with spontaneity.

Pierre Emmanuel, one of the poets who came up during the Second World War, was born during the earlier one, in 1916. His first book of poems, *Élégies,* was published in Brussels in 1940; his second, *Tombeau d'Orphée* (1941; *Tomb of Orpheus*), was published in unoccupied France at Villeneauve-lès-Avignon by the poet Pierre Seghers, who courageously edited the *Poésie* annuals during the war. The prolific Emmanuel had twelve other volumes of poetry published during the war, by Seghers and others; one of his most notable productions at this time was "Les Juifs" ("The Jews"), a long poem with the symbol of blood gushing through it: the blood of the Jews is the blood of Christ and the blood of the modern world. Frequently a religious poet, Emmanuel is the author of a candid autobiography, *Qui est cet Homme?* (1942; *Who Is This Man?*) and several postwar books of verse, including *Babel* (1952), *Visage Nuage* (1956; *Face Cloud*), and *Versant de l'âge* (1958; *Watershed of the Age*). One of his poems that catches an eternal situation and puts living people into it is "Érotique" ("Erotic"),

which begins with a naked woman singing as she dries
herself before a mirror:

In a room that the severe judge, a bed, fascinates,
The man is seated fully dressed with his eyes on the floor.

The animal that disturbs his soul, the ram,
Is it beating with desire of impatient fear?

Appear, sacred idol, against a red background!
Only a torch of gold moves between her thighs
And polishes with fires the armor of the naked breasts.

She, humble flesh, whose nakedness is homage,
Innocent, freezes and is disturbed by the face
Of shame that clothes this guilty unknown.

Often called the finest of the postwar French poets,
Yves Bonnefoy, born in 1923, is the author of *Du
Mouvement et de l'immobilité de Douve* (1953; *Of the
Movement and Immobility of Douve*), *Hier régnant
Désert* (1958; *Yesterday Desert Reigned*, winner of the
Prix Nouvelle Vague), and *Pierre écrite* (1959; *Written
Stone*). A philosophical poet, Bonnefoy often draws upon
mythology or Italian painting, but he can also draw upon
his own poetic resources, his investigation of meaning
through images, through seasoned concepts, as in "Douve
parle" ("Douve speaks"):

1

Sometimes, you said, walking at dawn
On the black paths,
I seem to partake of the hypnosis of stone,
I was blind like it.
But now this wind has come by which my comedies
Have clarified themselves in the act of dying.

I longed for the summer,
A raging summer to dry up my tears,
But now this cold has come that spreads in my limbs
And I was awakened and I suffered.

2

O fatal season,
O earth most bare like a blade!

I wanted summer,
Who has broken this iron in the old blood?

Really I was happy
Almost to the point of dying
My eyes lost, my hands open to the soiling
Of an eternal rain.

I cried out, I fought the wind with my face . . .
Why hate, why weep, I was alive,
The deep summer and the day reassured me.

In the third stanza, the poet cries out to have the word extinguished "In this low room where you re-unite with me. . . . May the cold be lifted up by my death and take a meaning."

There are numerous other younger poets who deserve at least to be mentioned, among them Claude Roy (*Un Seul Poème*, 1954; *A Single Poem*), Eugene Guillevic (*31 Sonnets*, 1954), Philippe Jaccottet (*l'Ignorant*, 1958), Alan Bosquet (*Deuxième Testament*, 1960; *Second Testament*), André du Bouchet (*Dans la Chaleur vacante*, 1962; *In the Empty Heat*), René Guy Cadou (*Le Cœur définitif*, 1962; *The Definitive Heart*), André Pieyre de Mandiargues (*Deuxième Belvédère*, 1962; *Second Belvedere*), Jean Follain (*Poèmes et prose choisis*, 1962; *Selected Poems and Prose*), Jean Grosjean (*Apocalypse*, 1962), Paul Gilson (*Énigmarelle*, 1963), Jacques Dupin (*Gravir*, 1963; *To Climb*), and Maurice Fombeure (*Quel est Ce Cœur?*, 1963; *What Is This Heart?*), but various others could be listed or examined also.

Among those mentioned immediately above, one of the most attractive is the Swiss-born Jaccottet, less influenced by surréalisme than many of his contemporaries, yet modern enough to recall Rilke and Valéry—though always with a voice of his own, as may be seen in one of his best-known sonnets, "Comme Je suis un étranger dans notre vie" ("As I am a Stranger in Our Life"). This love poem mingles the speaker's sensual approach to his beloved and his sensuous approach to the earth: "O fruits / so ripe, source of gold roads, gardens of ivy, / only to you do I speak, my absent one, my earth . . ."

Follain, often writing of pastoral or village scenes, makes small experiences memorable in prose poems such as this one from "Allées et venues" ("Comings and Goings" in the *Selected Poems and Prose*):

If the man walking should distracted kick at a violet-colored pebble, he is thinking over vague thoughts. The noises are certainly those of his adolescence. He passes before a shed where the cries of animals, because of the threatening sky, seem appeals made in vain. He walks on aimlessly, not like this farmer coming toward him, whom he must greet. So, to avoid him, he goes into a side road. The stones there are of another color, the hedgerows not so well trimmed, friendlier; the sky soon clears, open to the event.

Dupin's verse usually contains chaos, shattering, fragmentation, as in "Le Règne minéral" ("The Mineral Kingdom"):

In this country lightning makes stone grow.

On the peaks that command the gorges,
Ruined towers stand up
Like so many active mental torches
That revive on nights of great wind
The instinct of death in the quarryman's blood.

All the veins of granite
Will reveal themselves in his eyes.

But the poet states that the fire which speaks our tongue will never be cured of us: as in so much of Dupin's poetry, unceasing tension exists between the somatic in nature and the somatic of the human, an idea he frequently projects with abrupt juxtapositions and sudden imbalances, retaining always a concreteness of image and expression that gives his work its special vividness. With such poets as these, recent French verse is maintaining its living presence among the literary arts.

AFTER THE SECOND WORLD WAR, the drama flourished in France—it had even kept going during the occupation, and at the time of the liberation had burst forth in fresh strength. In the postwar period, the existentialiste plays and those of what has been called the theater of the absurd provided the most exciting drama, but traditional plays held their own, as always. Standard companies such as the Comédie française continued to operate as before, while independent troupes such as Jean-Louis Barrault's offered stimulating productions of both old and new plays.

Since playwriting in France is so closely bound up with producing, and even with the theaters where dramas are staged, the names of manager and actors and playhouses must often be mentioned in connection with individual comedies and tragedies. One of the great events in the history of the French theater, for example, occurred in 1946 when Jean-Louis Barrault and his wife and co-star, Madeleine Renaud, took over the Théâtre Marigny, near the gardens of the Champs-Élysées, opening with a highly successful production of André Gide's translation of *Hamlet*. They moved some years later to the Odéon, at the top of the rue de l'Odéon, on the left bank. Ludmilla Pitöeff, whose actor-manager husband had died in 1939, returned in 1946 to stage two of her former successes at the Comédie des Champs-Élysées: Henrik Ibsen's *Maison de poupée* (A *Doll's House*) and Paul Claudel's *l'Échange* (*The Exchange*). At the Mathurins, Marcel Herrand and Jean Marchat, producing foreign as well as French plays, proved to be exciting successors of the Pitoëffs. André Barsacq, continuing to be the producer of Anouilh, moved to the Atelier. Charles Dullin, who was to die in 1949, changed the name of the Théâtre de la Cité back to the Sarah Bernhardt. Louis Jouvet, who was to die in 1951, returned from South America to the Athénée, reviving not only Molière, but also Giraudoux (*Ondine* and *The Madwoman of Chaillot*). In 1951, Jean Vilar, who had been staging outdoor productions in Avignon, with the Palace of the Popes in the background, was made director of the Théâtre National Populaire, which plays in Paris and elsewhere: Vilar is known as an advocate of tréteau nu (bare stage) rather than of scène à l'italienne (Italian setting) productions, with more elaborate decoration. And so it goes, the theaters and personnel changing, as the following discussion of recent plays will sometimes indicate.

One of the postwar dramatists whose career dates back to the 1920's is Armand Salacrou, born at Rouen in 1899. He had the honor of seeing his first youthful plays, *Tour à terre* (*Tower on Land*) and *Le Pont de l'Europe* (*The Bridge of Europe*), produced on Christmas Eve, 1925 at the Théâtre de l'Œuvre by the great director Lugné-Poë. *The Bridge of Europe* is the story of Jêrome, a vagabond from Paris who is made king of an eastern European country but remains in love with the past, particularly with a Spanish dancer who hasn't returned his affection. The play, scrambled in its action, flares now and then into poetry, and has a generally surréaliste manner—like so many French authors of his generation, Salacrou has been influenced by both surréalisme and communism. Again in *Patchouli*, first produced in 1930 by Charles Dullin at the Atelier, Salacrou shows a man obsessed with the past; the play was a painful failure. Dullin had faith in Salacrou, however, and acted in his next play, *Atlas Hôtel*, which scored a success in 1931; but Salacrou didn't care much for this rather tricksy drama set in Africa. He came into his own as a playwright, after several more attempts, in

1935, when Lugné-Poë staged *l'Inconnue d'Arras* (*The Unknown Woman of Arras*, revived by Gaston Baty at the Comédie française in 1949). A man who learns that his wife has been unfaithful shoots himself, and although it takes him only a minute to die, the three acts of the play represent what rushes through his mind during that minute: the story of his life. *La Terre est ronde* (1938), directed by Dullin at the Atelier, concerns the hot religious fanaticism of Savanarola. Salacrou kept on writing and having his plays performed during the war, after which he wrote a forcibly realistic play, *Les Nuits de la colère* (1946; *The Nights of Anger*), which Barrault staged at the Atelier. Set in the cathedral city of Chartres, this is a drama of the résistance: a member of the underground who has blown up a train seeks refuge with his best friend, whose frightened wife, with her husband's connivance, informs a collaborator where the fugitive is. They foolishly believe that he will receive a fair trial, which he doesn't, and the friend who had hidden him is killed by the local résistance leader. He also shoots the collaborator, who in turn fatally wounds him, after which the play turns into a dialogue in which representatives of various attitudes defend their positions. In *l'Archipel Lenoir* (1947; *The Lenoir Archipelago*), Salacrou offers a satire on a family of wine manufacturers whose patriarch, at seventy-three, has attacked a young girl. When the family says it hopes to avoid trial, a relative by marriage— a Rumanian prince—says that this can be done only if the ancient ravisher dies. *Dieu le savait!* (1951; *God Saved Him!*) deals again with the résistance, actually with its aftermath; a woman whose husband the Germans have killed sees his opposition to them, and his bravery, as treachery to his family. *Le Miroir* (*The Mirror*) and *Une Femme trop honnête* (*A Woman Too Honest*), both produced in 1956, are like some of Salacrou's other plays in that they are somewhat trivial; and they show a lack of touch with a later public. But he has been an important playwright, sharing with Jean Anouilh the task of investigating the essence of disenchantment.

Anouilh's postwar career, after *Eurydice* and *Antigone*,

has been carried on with continuing success. His first two plays after the war were staged by Barsacq at the Atelier: *Roméo et Jeannette* (1946) and *l'Invitation au château* (1947; *The Invitation to the Château*, translated by Christopher Fry as *Ring Round the Moon*). In *Roméo et Jeannette*, three young people tangled in love work out their destiny against a fatal background. Frédéric, the Romeo of the occasion, becomes confused over his Juliet —two sisters named Julia and Jeannette. In love with Julia and intending to marry her, he insists upon meeting her family, which Julia doesn't want him to do because the members of the family are sloppy. When he does meet them, though he is properly horrified he falls in love with Jeannette, causing Julia to attempt suicide. Jeannette then promptly marries a wealthy man, but in her turn attempts suicide, walking into the sea, where Frédéric, seeing what she is doing, goes to death with her, making the play one of those the author has designated as pièces noires. But this melodramatic story of a triangle of star-crossed lovers is artistically unsatisfactory.

Anouilh's next attempt—featuring another Frédéric—is a far better play: *The Invitation to the Château* is full of lightness, with fantasy, the celebration of the counterfeit situation, and grotesquerie all dancing in twinkle-toe fashion across the stage, yet the comedy, one of the author's so-called pièces brillantes, has an underpaving of pessimism. Frédéric has an identical twin who is capable of envy and meanness, particularly after he learns that a girl who has rejected him, the wealthy Diana Messirsch-mann, is going to marry Frédéric after a quarrel with his brother, whom she really loves. But at a ball given at the château where the twins live with their aunt, Madame Desmermortes, a beautiful young girl appears, the dancer Isabelle, who is penniless. She has been imported by the disgruntled brother. Isabelle captivates everybody but Diana, who upon learning that the visitor has no social status, creates an uproar. The embarrassed Isabelle turns for sympathy to Frédéric, confusing him with the brother who had brought her, and Frédéric begins to fall in love with her. Diana's father offers Diana a huge sum of money to leave, but she tears up the bank notes; the wealthy man joins her, and they fling the pieces at the audience. When they have destroyed a fortune, Messirschmann asks her whether she is happy now, and she says, "No, are you?" He sadly replies that he isn't in the least happy, and he telephones his bankers to help him, but it appears that he is ruined: then, by a typical Anouilh twist, it turns out that because of actions taken by his agents—another Anouilh twist—Messirschmann is richer than before. Meanwhile, Frédéric and Isabelle realize that they are in love, and Diana goes back to the brother she really prefers. It is all improbable (the old twin story of Roman and Elizabethan comedy), but done with contagious gaiety above its fundamental seriousness. The arch artificiality of Anouilh is seen at its best or almost best, and the mischievous counterfeiting that is so much a part of this author's plays and characters is summed up by Madame Desmermortes who, watching Isabelle at the ball, says, "She's the only one who doesn't seem to be playing a part."

Ardèle (1948), one of the type that Anouilh calls pièces noires, is a black play indeed, although presented in a vaudeville style. It ends on the gruesome note of the suicide of a pair of idealistic, hunchbacked lovers. The drama is filled with shrieks, some uttered by a madwoman, some by a peacock, and there are a pair of corrupt children whose behavior reflects that of the adults whom they know. In *Colombe* (1951), a pretty little flower girl has married the simple-hearted Julien, son of a famous actress who refuses to speak to her son. But when he is leaving for military service, he brings Colombe to his mother for protection, and the girl soon becomes an actress with a flock of hot-eyed admirers. She succumbs to Julien's cynical brother Paul, and a whole world of sly corruption opens out which makes poor Julien's trustfulness seem naïf indeed. In *La Valse des toréadors* (1952; *The Waltz of the Toreadors*), directed by Roland Pietri at the Champs-Élysées (it appeared in New York in translation, with Sir Ralph Richardson as the star), one of the characters from *Ardèle* reappears: the erotically inclined, middle-aged Général Saint-Pé. The general, who is not in love with his insane wife (in the former play he was having an affair with the housemaid), in *The Waltz* meets an aging former sweetheart, Ghislaine de Saint-Euverte, whom he had loved in his youth. Indeed it was, though platonic, the only love of his life. But the later meeting brings about savage complications, with Ghislaine and the madwoman simultaneously attempting suicide. But Ghislaine eventually runs away with the general's secretary, with whom the general's homely daughters have flirted, not realizing that he is their half-brother, the general's illegitimate son. At the end, the general, one of Anouilh's few truly sympathetic characters, is left with his mad wife and a new maid, to whom he can make love to relieve some of the darkness of the world.

L'Alouette (1953; *The Lark*) was directed by Anouilh himself at the Théâtre Montparnasse, with Joan of Arc played by Suzanne Plon (Dorothy Tutin appeared in the part in London, and Julie Harris in New York). As in the Anouilh version of *Antigone*, a young woman defies the state in *The Lark*, but not with the tense effectiveness that characterized the earlier drama. Joan is more the French peasant girl in this play than in other stage pieces about her; the action opens with the trial, then presents flashbacks of Joan's earlier life; the ending evades the burning of Joan, for the play must end happily. The total effect is one of fine theatricalism, but not of power, even of credible satire. Anouilh, after several other dramas, turned again to history for *Becket ou l'honneur de Dieu* (1959; *Becket, or the Honor of God*), also staged by Pietri at the Montparnasse. (It was played in New York with Laurence Olivier as Becket and Anthony Quinn as Henry II, and filmed with Richard Burton and Peter O'Toole in these leading parts). Once more, Anouilh has written of a conflict between the beliefs of an individual and those of a representative of the state. When Becket discovers the honor of God, the king who has been his friend becomes his enemy. The play begins with Henry II stripping himself naked before the tomb of the churchman who had been murdered because the king has cried out against him. The story then sweeps back to show the time when Becket was the lord chancellor and his royal friend's fellow libertine. But when the king made Becket the Archbishop of Canterbury, the man changed to fit the position, and the king was enraged, assuming the attitude of a rejected lover. He permitted the Bishop of London to draw up an accusation to the effect that Becket, in contempt of the king and at the prompting of an evil spirit, presided over a sacrilegious mass. Henry and Becket meet for the last time in life on horseback on a plain raked by an icy wind:

KING You know that I am king, and must act the part of king. What do you want me to do? Are you hoping that I'll weaken?

BECKET No. That would leave me prostrate.

KING Do you expect then to win me over by force?

BECKET You are the strong one.

KING To convince me?

BECKET No, not that. I shall not try to convince you. I have only to say no.

KING But you must be logical, Becket!

BECKET No, it's not necessary, my liege. One can only do—absurdly—what one has been entrusted to do—up to the end.

As the play ends, King Henry has himself flogged by four monks, corresponding to the four knights who killed Becket; after he puts his robes back on, he tells a baron who comes in that hereafter in this kingdom he wants Becket to be regarded as a saint. This play was far superior to *The Lark* as drama, with a skillful resolution of its conflicts and a legerdemain of irony prevailing throughout. It demonstrated once again that Anouilh is the master of a certain type of French theater, in which the humorously fanciful and the clankingly realistic can occasionally work together, although there is always a pervasive sense of falsity. In *La Foire d'empoigne* (1962; *The Failure of Seizing*, possibly a pun on a word literally meaning both market fair and diarrhea besides failure), Anouilh gave a stern caricature of the Napoleon of the time just before Waterloo, a play preceded by a shorter one, *l'Orchestre*, a comedy about women musicians who play at resorts.

In France, many more novelists write for the theater than in other countries. There are, for example, the plays of Jules Romains, Georges Duhamel, Roger Martin du Gard, Henry de Montherlant, and François Mauriac, which were extensively staged before the war. Some of those of Montherlant and Mauriac, however, belong to the period now under consideration, for example Mauriac's *Les mal aimés* (1945; *The Badly Loved*), *Passage du mal* (1948; *Passage of the Evil One*), and *Le Feu sur la terre* (1951; *The Fire on the Earth*), all discussed earlier and characterized as less successful than his novels. Montherlant's postwar drama, *Demain il fera jour* (1949; *Tomorrow It Will Be Dawn*) has also been mentioned earlier as the sequel to one of his wartime plays. Montherlant has since written frequently for the theater; his *Le Maître de Santiago* (1948; *The Master of Santiago*), written in 1945, is set in sixteenth-century Spain, the country of Montherlant's ancestry. His inspiration for the play came in 1933, when he read that some of the older members of the Spanish nobility believed that the discovery of the new world was a disaster for Spain.

In the play, the true master of the Order of Santiago — of which the king is the nominal head — is Don Alvaro Dabo, who is disgusted with the world and decides to renounce it, taking his eighteen-year-old daughter, Mariana, with him into religious solitude. When one of the other noblemen tries to trick him by telling him that the king has ordered a group of them, including Alvaro, to go to the new world to mine the gold that is there, Mariana shows what stuff she is made of: she was in on the strategy, which would have enabled her to marry while her father was away, but at the last moment she reveals to

Alvaro that the king gave him no such command. She too is renouncing the world. As her father tells her,

> Our blood shall not mingle with any other. There will be no man who will turn and turn you in his arms. And no children will soil me, no one will betray me: with you, everything of mine reaches its end cleanly. The last! We shall be the last! What power in that word, the last, which opens out to the sublime void.

This is a play of hardness, of rigor, of renunciation. Its author was not perhaps recommending a course of action, but merely presenting a dramatic portrait. He has spoken of Alvaro as being saturnine.

In *Celles qu'on prend dans ses bras* (1950; *Those One Holds in his Arms*), Montherlant shows an old collector of antiques, Ravier, long loved in vain by a woman slightly older than he, who is himself obsessed with the young Christine Villancy. She eludes him until after he has saved her father from disgrace, and then she offers herself to him. He hesitates, then agrees to take her, although admitting it is a low act: "Nothing is lower nor more vulgar than the way in which I accept you, but nearly everyone who is born is of impure origin." The play was unsuccessful on the stage, and the charge was brought against it that Christine's act was unreal—a ridiculous criticism, as Montherlant made plain when he stated that, before writing the scene, he had interviewed many young women who without exception said that such an action was within the range of Chrisine's character. In that year of 1950, Montherlant also brought out *Malatesta*, which he had written at Grasse in 1943–44. It was produced at the Marigny by Barrault, who played the leading rôle of Sigismond Malatesta, for which he has admitted he is perhaps too frail. The play is full of the energetic motion and hot colors of the Renaissance. Malatesta, afraid that the Pope wants to take the town of Rimini away from him, plans to kill the Holy Father, but can't force himself to carry out his plan. He is imprisoned in the Vatican until his wife obtains his release, but back in Rimini a

supposed friend murders him. The play opens on a
vigorous note when Malatesta, in a duel with his fencing
instructor, kills him after crying out, "This time I castrate
you! I castrate you and eat them for dinner!"—hearty fare,
even for a stage Renaissance.

La Ville dont le prince est un enfant (The Town
Where the Prince is a Child) was published in 1951 but
not produced on the stage (except for one scene played at
the Biarritz Casino in 1952, some private readings, and a
recording made in 1958); the Archbishop of Paris advised
Montherlant not to let the complete drama be produced,
apparently because of the emotions two boy actors would
have to exhibit on the stage. The play, somewhat reminiscent of Montherlant's early fiction, takes its title from
Ecclesiastes 10:16, "Woe to thee, O land, when thy king
is a child." A boy of sixteen and one of fourteen are in
love, in a religious school in Paris. Sexuality doesn't
intrude onstage, but the relationship is an erotic one, and
a priest becomes involved, entangling matters further.
Montherlant's next play to be staged was Port-Royal
(1954), performed at the Comédie française; it concerns a
group of nuns in the seventeenth century, at the time the
church was attempting to suppress Jansenism, that doctrine which taught predestination rather than salvation
through good works. Montherlant in his quietly plotted
but forcefully "psychological" play, doesn't deal with the
philosophical questions involved, but rather with the
conflict between the ecclesiastical authorities and the
Jansenist nuns of Port-Royal. Montherlant announced
this as his last play, but he has continued to turn out
work for the theater, including Brocéliande (1956), Don
Juan (1958), and Le Cardinal d'Espagne (1960; The
Cardinal of Spain). In the comedy Brocéliande, a timid
little bourgeois named Persilès comes to believe that he is
a descendant of Saint-Louis and suddenly adopts a holier-
than-thou attitude and regards himself as being above his
fellowmen. Don Juan, with the legend treated farcically,
was a heavy failure. In The Cardinal of Spain, the
protagonist Ximénez is torn between the desire for power
and the desire for withdrawal, and the struggle between

the two of them pull him to his death. Montherlant, who has stated that he hasn't tried to prove anything in his plays, has in the best of them given the modern theater a number of excitingly wrought stories and some grand moments of dramatic intensity.

Among other fiction writers who have turned out dramatic pieces—including Georges Bernanos, Julien Green, and Marcel Aymé—Bernanos didn't write directly for the stage, but a film script he prepared was dramatized for production in the theater before it appeared on the screen. This was *Dialogues des Carmélites* (*Dialogues of the Carmelites*), which was Bernanos's last work shortly before his death in 1948. It was based on a story of the time of the French revolution, Gertrud von Le Fort's novella of 1931, *Die Letzte am Schafott* (*The Last on the Scaffold*). Adapted for the stage from Bernanos's scenario, it became, in the hands of Albert Béguin and Marcelle Tassencourt, what Wallace Fowlie (in *Dionysus in Paris*) has called "outside the dramas of Claudel, the most moving religious play of the century." It was produced at the Hébertot in 1950 with Hélène Bourdan in the leading rôle of Blanche de la Force, the young French aristocrat who is terrified of even the smallest manifestations of life, and above all of the violence of the revolution. When the Carmelite nuns with whom Blanche is associated take vows of martyrdom, she runs away. Yet, on the day when the Jacobins are going to guillotine the members of Blanche's particular group, she appears in time to be the last at the scaffold. The ending is a fine stroke of theater; the nuns, singing the "Salve Regina" and then the "Veni Creator," walk one at a time up to the platform, and the offstage crash of the falling blade is heard; as the number of the women diminishes, their voices are reduced, at last to three, then to two, and at last to one; but suddenly a new, strong voice is heard as Blanche appears out of the crowd, steps forward, and then mounts the steps; the blade makes its last smashing sound, then the curtain comes down in a tense silence. The original script of Bernanos was finally filmed in 1960.

Julien Green's first play, *Sud* (1953; *South*) was based

on his unfinished novel, Les Pays lointains (Distant Countries). In this play he returns to one of his favorite settings, the American South, this time to a plantation house in the Carolinas just as the Civil War is starting. A young officer who is visiting the family there meets another young man, a neighboring planter, who is in love with one of the girls in the family, to whom the lieutenant suddenly proposes. He antagonizes the planter into a duel, in which he lets himself be killed: not realizing the capacity of his own nature, he had fallen in love with the young planter, and elects to face suicide rather than himself. In l'Ennemi (1954; The Enemy), Green goes back to the French revolution and a huge and solitary château, partly damaged by the fighting, where Élisabeth de Silleranges lives with her impotent husband, Philippe. She has become the mistress of Philippe's brother, Jacques, though she doesn't love him. Then Pierre, the bastard half-brother of the Silleranges', appears after leaving his monastery before taking the final vows. He fascinates Élisabeth, to whom this diabolical figure offers an escape from "the inexorable boredom which forms the basis of all human life and of which the passions, the most delicate pleasures, even suffering, can distract us only for an instant." Pierre is really the servant of the enemy, the prince of earth—Satan—and yet, through the mysticism of sinning with him, Élisabeth is brought to a revelation of God, a kind of salvation by mistake. Green's third play, l'Ombre (1956; The Shadow), shows an Englishman, Charles Anderson, haunted by the shadow of his first wife, whom he had believed was unfaithful to him with his best friend. In a darkly ironic scheme, he engages this friend to kill her. When, years later, Anderson learns that she had remained faithful to him, he kills himself. Here is the dramatically and psychologically somber world of Green's novels. This religious author is apparently trying to help point the way to good in the world by exposing its ambient evil.

Another writer of fiction who has turned to the theater, Marcel Aymé, injects into his plays the same kind of satire, particularly on small-town life, which characterizes his novels and short stories. In 1947 he brought out a comedy written fifteen years earlier, *Lucienne et le boucher* (*Lucienne and the Butcher*), which fiercely caricatured the daily life of a provincial city. Aymé's finest play is *Clérambard* (1950), in which the impoverished Count Clérambard tyrannizes over a family that has to labor endlessly at indoor looms in order to earn a few francs. But he decides to become a saint after St. Francis has appeared to him. So, a character in the tradition of Alfred Jarry's bullying schoolmaster in *Ubu-Roi* suddenly tries to become Franciscan. As part of this particular type of holiness, Clérambard determines that his pimply son shall marry a prostitute. One of the points of the play is that saintliness has its own tyrannies, and that saints are difficult persons to have in the house. In *La Tête des autres* (1952; *The Brains of Others*), Aymé's savage weapon of satire turned against the legal profession. Valorin, convicted of murder, manages to escape from court and hide in a house which turns out to be the home of the prosecutor, Maillard, the first of the play's remarkable coincidences, but the kind of trickery French audiences usually don't object to. This coincidence is followed by one even more striking, for when Valorin enters Maillard's parlor he finds the missing witness in his case: he had based his defense upon the fact that he had spent the night of the crime in a hotel with a woman he had picked up on the streets—and suddenly she is before him again. But Maillard tells the woman, Roberte, not to bother herself by even answering Valorin's questions, which to an old cross-examiner seem ridiculous. But Valorin persists, describing the marks on the woman's body and even her type of garters and girdle; in an emphatically Gallic scene he suddenly leans over and raises Roberte's dress to show her black-and-yellow striped garters. But the shocks in the play are not confined to this scene of climax. Audiences in other countries would be shocked to hear a woman say on the stage, "an officer told me the other day that in the Tunisian wasteland, where the soldiers are deprived of feminine company, they make up for it on their mules. It's a thing I'd like very much to see." In *Les Oiseux de lune* (1955; *Moon Birds*), Aymé plays with the idea that a man can change others into birds. A miserable, persecuted little schoolteacher, who discovers that he has this power, one day uses it against his mother-in-law, his outrageous pupils, the police, and spoilsports in general, putting them all in a cage. *La Mouche bleue* (1957; *The Blue Fly*) is a satire on Americans for their worship of money and their terror of sex. Aymé believes that satire should be fierce.

The farces of Jacques Audiberti (1899–1965) often become parody but rarely extreme satire such as Aymé's. Arriving in Paris from his native Antibes in 1925, Audiberti fell under the spell of the surréalistes, in 1930 bringing out his first volume of poems, *l'Empire et la trappe* (*The Empire and the Trap*). After the war he became a novelist with such books as *Abraxas* (1947), beginning in the theater with *Quoat-Quoat* (1946), the story of a primitive Mexican god. He followed this with *Le Mal Court* (1947; *The Evil Court*), a philosophical farce dealing with Occidental-Oriental moral problems, a play whose most striking scene is the princess' strip tease before the cardinal. In *Les Naturels du Bordelais* (1953; *The Bordeaux Country Natives*), Audiberti introduces a supreme charlatan in La Bequilleuse, who at different times is a successful poet, a peddler of aphrodisiacs, and a high-ranking police officer; but these transformations are in keeping with the spirit of the play, whose characters become critics. Audiberti has an emphatic originality, but he is too often tricksy, too extreme in his attempts to create the fantastic out of the ordinary. In 1962 he launched a popular success with *Pomme, Pomme, Pomme* (*Apple, Apple, Apple*), his modern version of the Adam and Eve story.

Audiberti's exact contemporary, also born in 1899, Marcel Achard, has been writing plays over a longer period. An acknowledged master of the light stroke, Achard scored one of his earlier successes with a play based on an old popular song, *Malborough s'en va-t-en guerre* (1924; *Marlborough Goes to War*). Over the years Achard's plays have been staged by France's finest directors, including Jean-Louis Barrault (who revived *Marlborough* at the Marigny in 1950), Charles Dullin, Louis Jouvet, and others. Jouvet, Michel Simon, and Valentine Tessier starred in Achard's *Jean de la lune* (*John from the Moon*) in 1929. Achard's *Le Corsaire* (1938; *The Pirate*), produced at the Champs-Élysées by Jouvet, provided in English translation one of the most popular comedies of Alfred Lunt and Lynn Fontanne in the United States. Achard has gone on writing plays with great public success, superficial as many of them have been. His *Patate* (1957) was about the relationship of two men, a scoundrel and his patate, or fall guy. When the patate learns that the scoundrel, who has grown rich, has seduced the fall guy's adopted daughter, complications ensue, and the men's rôles are reversed; but the patate doesn't know how to behave as anything else. During the 1962 season, Achard was represented by two plays on Parisian stages: *Turlututu* (starring the nightclub favorite Robert Lamureux) and a musical comedy for which he wrote the libretto, *La Polka des lampions* (*The Polka of the Lighted Lamps*, which could also be translated as *The Polka of the Cocked Hats*). Two other writers of comedies who should be mentioned are André Roussin, born 1911, author of *Le Petite Hutte* (1950; *The Little Hut*), an international light-comedy success, and Gabriel Arout, who wrote a light play with Maupassant overtones, *La Dame de trèfle* (1952; *The Queen of Clubs*), in which a man cannot decide whether the beautiful woman he meets in her own respectable parlor is the same beautiful woman he encounters at a brothel—as of course she is.

Henri Pichette, half-American, born in 1924, was influenced by the surréalistes in his early work, *Les Epiphanies* (1947). A poet, he composes for a lyric theater, as in *Nucléa*, a play about the atomic age, written in classic French alexandrine lines. Another poet of the French theater is the Lebanese, Georges Schehadé, born in 1910, whose first play, *Monsieur Bob'le* (1951), created one of those uproars of which Parisians are so capable. Produced by Georges Vitaly in the city's smallest theater, La Huchette, *Monsieur Bob'le* was violently attacked by the press. Bob'le is a character at once simple and complicated, divided between indifference and engagement, yet a man with a profound influence upon his fellow townsmen. Schehadé's second play, *La Soirée des proverbes* (1954; *The Evening Party of Proverbs*), came out under the banner of Barrault, who directed and acted in it at the Marigny. It is a fantastic and symbolic comedy of youth and age in which old people confront their once-young selves, disastrously. The third play of Schehadé, *Histoire de Vasco* (1956; *Story of Vasco*), also staged and performed by Barrault, is set in the middle of the last century, during a war in an unnamed country. A pacifist barber, Vasco, is drawn into the conflict and killed. Several influential critics growled that the play was antimilitaristic and that, since French soldiers were dying in Algeria, *Vasco* should be censored.

With Schehadé and Pichette, we find ourselves in what some French critics call the poetic antitheater. But we have not left French drama, since the later existential plays are yet to be dealt with, and the so-called theater of the absurd is also to be discussed. At this point, however, something should be said about a few of the Belgian dramatists who write in French. The best known of these is Michel de Ghelderode, who died in 1962 at the age of sixty-four.

The Belgians cause a certain amount of confusion because they have two literatures, one written in Dutch (Fleming) and one in French (Walloon), corresponding respectively to Germanic and Latin origins. Flemish prevails in the north, Walloon in the south, with both languages used in the capital, Brussels. Michel de Ghelderode, whose work was discovered by the Parisians after the Second World War, wrote in French, though his plays were in most cases first performed, in translation, by a Flemish troupe, the Vlaamse Volkstoneel.

His somewhat older contemporary, Fernand Crommelynck, born in 1885, also used the French tongue. Crommelynck's *Le Cocu magnifique* (1920; *The Magnificent
Cuckold*) is a play about jealousy, a play which its author
called a farce. It presents a husband (whose double nature
is emblemized by two actors on the stage) so suspicious of
his beautiful wife that he at last forces her to take lovers,
and then refuses to believe in her infidelity, just as he
refuses to face the reality of the situation when she at last
leaves him for a dull man. The play shocked audiences in
both Brussels and Paris, but was successful enough to
enable Crommelynck to give up his career as an actor and
devote all his time to writing. *Tripes d'or* (*Golden
Tripes*) was well received when Louis Jouvet presented it
at the Comédie des Champs-Élysées in 1925, and since it
is about a miser who destroys himself physically by
swallowing his gold, the play is also popular, under-
standably, in the Soviet Union. Crommelynck, a master of
words, has continued to be highly esteemed in France; his
Le Chevalier à la lune ou Sir John Falstaff (1954; *The
Moon Horseman, or Sir John Falstaff*) is based on
Shakespeare.

Michel de Ghelderode was a solitary who lived for the
greater part of his life in a room full of dress-shop
dummies, macabre marionettes, old armor, and seashells.
In 1951 he was badgered, at a time when he was ill, into
making some self-revelations in radio discussions, later
published as *Les Entretiens d'Ostende* (1956; *The Ostend
Interviews*). In the course of these he said that although
he had two brothers and a sister, his true sister was
solitude, his partner and pure love: "I say it once more:
my fate is to be alone."

Born at Ixelles, in Brabant, de Ghelderode was the son
of the principal clerk of the Archives Genérales, a man
who believed that in the modern world of conformity the
best occupation a man could have was that of civil
servant. In boyhood, his nonconforming son Michel built
for himself what he called a second life, a dark life which
he kept hidden like a treasure. When he was sixteen, a

serious illness took him away from his classical studies, and he began producing poems, which he later lost; he also kept a journal. But he didn't seriously take up writing until 1916–17. The puppet performances of the Belgian marketplaces had always fascinated him, and the elements of their plays are often reflected in his own work, along with his lifelong enthusiasm for such novels as *Don Quixote* and *Til Ulenspiegel*.

Michel de Ghelderode wrote more than fifty plays. After several of his early works (beginning in 1919) were presented in Brussels and Antwerp, his *La Mort du Doctor Faust* (*The Death of Doctor Faust*) was staged in Paris in 1928, at the Théâtre Art et Action, but de Ghelderode was not yet to capture the French. Meanwhile, he went on writing the plays that were eventually to be widely recognized, such as *Barabbas*, first produced in 1929, apparently in Antwerp, and *Pantagleize*, first performed in a Flemish translation, also 1929, in Brussels. *Barabbas* gives an unusual view of Christ's death, as seen from a drama centered in the criminal Barabbas, who was turned loose at the mob's request when Christ was sent to the cross on Calvary. That cross and the two that rise beside it overshadow a carnival ground where, amid the celebrating crowd, Barabbas is stabbed the moment Christ dies on the hill above. In the other play, Pantagleize is de Ghelderode's Everyman, and by the time he reaches his fortieth birthday, as the play opens, he is a misfit in utilitarian society. Going to a café filled with revolutionaries—it is the first of May—Pantagleize says "What a lovely day!" This phrase is the signal for a revolution to start, as one does, catching up Pantagleize in its mad events and eventually leading him to his death.

These two plays may serve as representative of de Ghelderode who, though he wrote in French, and in a wildly poetic French, was Flemish in spirit. His plays not only have their puppet-play elements, but also phases of the macabre, the supernatural, the carnal, the monstrous. The drama which attracted the attention of the French public to de Ghelderode in 1947 was *Hop Signor!*, a violent drama of lust in which a married woman who is a virgin is attracted to an executioner, who is also a virgin. Both are fascinated by his function, the legal murder, and their sexual ardor goes into the lust of killing. As the author draws his dramatic net tight, there is no solution possible for the situation other than having the executioner, Larose, behead the girl, Marguerite.

But if de Ghelderode wrote grimly, often in a manner whose confusion of action and whose whirl of scenes suggested German expressionism, and if his closed-off life seemed not merely antisocial but grim too, he nonetheless was not a prophet of despair, as he showed in *The Ostend Interviews:*

> Men are not lovely, not often, and it's very well that they are not even more ugly; but I believe in *Man*, and I think that this can be felt in my work. I don't despair of him, and I find him very interesting, capable of everything—and of its opposite.

3 THE CONTINUATION
OF EXISTENTIALISME

1 A Review of a Doctrine

Existentialisme as imaginative literature began in France just before the Second World War, and continued through that period, particularly in the plays and novels of Jean-Paul Sartre. Critics have traced existentialiste tendencies in the work of earlier imaginative writers— Fyodor Dostoevsky, Rainer Maria Rilke, and Franz Kafka, for example—but the present trend, as virtually an official school, began with Sartre, with his novel *La Nausée* (1938; *Nausea*), his short stories in *Le Mur* (1939; *The Wall*), as well as his plays *Les Mouches* (1943; *The Flies*) and *Huis-clos* (1944; *No Exit*) and his philosophical volume *l'Être et le néant* (1943; *Being and Nothingness*).

Many present-day writers use existential concepts, for the philosophy has become one of the fashions of the time; but the school of Sartre is a small one.

Several German professors are important as part of the background of Sartre's thinking, notably Edmund Husserl, who died in 1938, and Martin Heidegger, who at this writing is still alive. Karl Jaspers, likewise still living, is also important in the existentialiste movement, of which he has his own branch, and it is important to mention Friedrich Nietzsche, who died in 1900. But the true ancestor of the movement is the Danish writer, Søren Kierkegaard (1813–55), author of *Enten-Eller* (1843; *Either / Or*), *Frygt og Baeven* (1843; *Fear and Trembling*), *Stadier paa Livets Vej* (1845; *Stages on Life's*

Way), *Afstunde unvidensakabelig Efterskrift* (1846; *Concluding Unscientific Postscript*), *Sygdommen til Døden* (1849; *The Sickness Unto Death*), and other tests which have become the scriptures of the movement. Kierkegaard, a strong antirationalist, reacted against the philosophy of Hegel, which he apparently didn't know thoroughly. He opposed its logic of resolving contrarieties through a dialectical method tending toward systematization. Kierkegaard knew far more about Christianity than he knew about Hegel, for he was brought up under the sternly religious influence of a father who had felt guilty about God since childhood. Søren Kierkegaard opposed orthodox and organized Christianity. He posited the remoteness of God and stressed the need of man to recognize himself through his individuality. Man must make decisions on his own: no immediate element in his world can help him. All is reduced to the self and its responsibility for action.

Heidegger, Jaspers, Husserl, and other German philosophers, as well as the Swiss theologian Karl Barth, have in their different ways adapted Kierkegaard's ideas to modern thought. Some of these adaptations are religious, others atheistic. More than most philosophers, Heidegger uses Nietzsche, who said that God was dead. Heidegger, a member of the atheist wing, abdicated his responsibilities as a philosopher to become a zealous Nazi in 1933. As rector of Freiburg University, he barred his old friend and master Husserl from teaching there because Husserl was a Jew. Jaspers, who prefers not to speak of existentialisme but rather of Existenzphilosophie, Existenz Philosophy, also draws upon Nietzsche, but Jaspers is a Catholic; during the Nazi régime he quietly but firmly resisted the prevailing doctrines, and after the war he was one of the first to confront the problem of German culpability, in *Die Schuldfrage* (1946; *The Question of Guilt*).

There have been other Christian existentialistes, including the French philosopher and playwright, Gabriel Marcel, who prefers to be known as a neo-Socratic. Sartre staunchly places himself among the atheists. Sartre's character Antoine Roquentin in *Nausea* (1938) came to an existential realization at the end of the novel, specifically the discovery of his own existence. This book worked out one of the existential tenets: existence comes before essence. That is, the objective self-realization of the data of consciousness precedes functioning, usage, or a concept capable of definition. In *Being and Nothingness*, whose ideas he worked out in prison camp, Sartre thoroughly examined the concept of mauvaise foi, or bad faith, which has various manifestations. One of these, as the atheist existentialistes see it, is man's search for a God that doesn't exist. Rather than indulge in such misguided activity, these philosophers believe, man should find his identification in his own existence.

The atheist existentialistes have taken over from Kierkegaard not only the idea that man is an alien in the world, but also that he suffers from Angst, or anguish. This is caused by man's confronting the void of nothingness, which produces a vision of the absurdity of life. But man must create for himself a rational attitude, must become engagé (engaged). Sartre has said that adherents of Christianity often project their own despair upon the existentialistes, and he asserts that this is wrong because existentialisme is a philosophy of action and hope through which man can most truly realize his freedom.

2 *The Later Career of Sartre*

Sartre's essays and imaginative work have continued to embody this type of thinking. After the war he began a tetralogy of novels, of which he published three volumes and the fragment of a fourth. This series, *Les Chemins de la liberté* (*The Roads to Freedom*), is made up of *l'Âge de raison* (1945; *The Age of Reason*), *Le Sursis* (1945; *The Reprieve*), and *La Mort dans l'âme* (1949; *Death in the Soul*, translated as *Troubled Sleep*, also translated as *Iron in the Soul*). Parts of the fourth volume, *La Dernière Chance* (*The Last Chance*), appeared in the journal *Les Temps modernes*; (*Modern Times*) as *Drôle d'amitié* (*Strange Friendship*) in the issues of November and December, 1949.

These novels, which depict France in the late 1930's and early 1940's, deal with groups. In the second volume, *The Reprieve*, Sartre seems almost to be making use of Jules Romains's unanimisme, and of the mass-novel techniques John Dos Passos developed in *Manhattan Transfer* and *U.S.A.* Sartre in the second volume of his sequence makes extensive use of simultanéisme, the tele-scoping of events which occurs in the work of such writers as James Joyce and in attempts in modernistic painting to suggest several occurrences going on at the same time on a single canvas (as in some of Pablo Picasso's work). Sartre in *The Reprieve* often jumps from one person's point of view to another's in a single passage, or from one point in time to another. As an example of Sartre's use of simultanéisme, events occurring at the same moment in different places, consider a passage in the second chapter in *The Reprieve*, dated "Saturday, September 24":

> At Crévilly, at exactly six o'clock, Daddy Croulard went into the gendarmerie and knocked on the door of the office. He thought: "They woke me up." He thought of saying to them: "Why have I been awakened?" Hitler was asleep, Chamberlain was asleep, whistling snores through his nose, Daniel was sitting on his bed pouring with sweat, and he thought, "It was only a nightmare!"
> "Come in," the gendarmerie lieutenant said. "Ah, it's you, Daddy Croulard? Well, you'll have to start getting busy."
> Ivich groaned faintly and turned on her side.
> "The boy woke me up," Daddy Croulard said.

Here we have a broad canvas with various events taking place across distances. Daddy Croulard is an unimportant character, a man wearing wooden shoes who posts notices in the town; he has been summoned to put up (mistak-enly) posters announcing mobilization. He asks, "Why have I been awakened?"—in most novels, the next sen-tence, beginning, "Hitler was asleep, Chamberlain was asleep," would be Croulard's stream of consciousness: the statesmen were still sleeping, so why must the billboard man be wakened up? But Sartre has not intended this to read so: he is flashing to Hitler and Chamberlain as they lie asleep in Germany. And, in the same sentence, Daniel is sitting on his bed, sweating after a nightmare. Daniel is nowhere near Hitler and Chamberlain, for he is (we learn later) in the Midi town of Sauveterre. Then suddenly a short paragraph is devoted to Ivich, who is having an uneasy sleep; readers of the preceding volume, *The Age of Reason*, will recall her as the girl of Russian derivation who has gone back to the northern French town of Laon, where her father lives. Then, in the next sentence, Daddy Croulard is back again. This is a technique used throughout the book; it is clever, and imitative, here at best a tour de force, but neatly executed.

Another example may be given in a single sentence: "Tears of anger came into Milan's eyes, and Daniel turned toward Marcelle—*my* wife, *my* future, the only one that remains for me, since the world has decided for Peace." Here is simultanéisme indeed, for the Milan of the first phrase in the sentence is Milan Hlinka, in a Czechoslovakian town, and the anger that brings tears to his eyes is anger at a group of arrogant Sudeten Germans; but after that first phrase of just a few words, only a comma separates Milan from Daniel Sereno, who is with his wife in that southern French town of Sauveterre. Sartre says that he doesn't believe in Bergsonian time, that he is aware of durée, of Bergson's concept of flowing time, only when he wants to be; these examples of his use of simultanéisme will show how he employs time in another way in his group novels.

The first of them, *The Age of Reason*, deals with such matters more simply; it is a third-person story which often moves abruptly from scene to scene or, as Sartre observes in the course of the narrative, "time passed with sudden and fateful jolts." The story takes place in two days of June, 1938. The central figure of the story is Mathieu Delarue, a teacher of philosophy, who learns with a shock that his mistress, Marcelle Duffit, is pregnant. A doctor about to leave for the United States agrees to perform an abortion for 4,000 francs—about $160 in American currency then—which is beyond the range of Mathieu, who fails to borrow it from his brother and then from his friend Daniel Sereno. He finally steals the money from Lola Montero, an aging nightclub singer. She is dazed from an overdose of drugs she has taken after a quarrel with her lover, one of Mathieu's students, the Russian-born Boris Serguine.

In this complicated plot, Mathieu is attracted by Boris' sister, the blonde Ivich, who has a broad, pale, sensual, and girlish face "like the moon among the clouds." One night at a café, Ivich impulsively cuts her hand with a knife. Mathieu imitates her, and later they rub the wounds together, mingling their blood.

Mathieu hasn't realized that Marcelle wants to have a baby, a point she confides to Daniel, who is a homosexual. Daniel has tried to kill himself, but couldn't carry out the preliminaries to his suicide by drowning his beloved cats in the Seine. At the end of the story, Mathieu, in order to save Boris from being wrongly accused of stealing the 4,000 francs, returns it to Lola. Daniel, who has tried to unsex himself with a razor and has as usual ended in futility, offers to marry Marcelle and give her child a father. He confesses his homoeroticism to Mathieu, but says he can keep a woman satisfied and will be a dutiful husband. Here is the existential choice, however "wrong" in direction it has been: Daniel has, in following these particular sexual inclinations deliberately selected the life that will lead him to guilt and toward attempts at suicide and castration. Another existentialiste portrait is that of the Communist Brunet, who calls Mathieu—the intellectual who wanted to fight for the loyalists in the Spanish war but couldn't in any sense become engaged—"the social traitor." Brunet, who will become more important in the later parts of the story, emphasizes, by his very presence in the first novel, Mathieu's nonexistential detachment.

The style of this first book is almost chastely classical, almost as unfurnished—to translate the French word démeublé—as Stendhal's. An occasional metaphor floats out, such as the one previously quoted which compares Ivich's face to the moon among the clouds, and there is a vision of the Louvre arcades, seen from a taxi window, "like large doves in flight"; but for the most part the language is plain. At the end of the book, there has been a tumult of scenes in Mathieu's room—Ivich has gone off to her town in the provinces, Mathieu has returned the money to Lola, and Daniel has arrived to make his confession and announce that he will marry Marcelle. Then Mathieu is left alone:

> He shut the window of the balcony and turned back into the room. Ivich's scent still hung in the air. He breathed it in and thought over the day of tumult. "Much ado about nothing," he reflected. About nothing: this life had been given to him for nothing, he was nothing, and he would never change: this was the way he had been made. He took off his shoes and sat, without moving, on the arm of the chair: he could feel in his throat the yellow-gold, sugared sharpness of rum. He yawned: he had finished his day's work, and he had finished with his youth. Well-seasoned moralities already discreetly offered their help. There was disillusioned epicureanism, grinning tolerance, resignation, plain seriousness, stoicism—everything by which a man might savor, expertly, the failure of his life. He took off his coat and started to unfasten his tie. He yawned again as he repeated to himself, "It's true, it's completely true: I have arrived at the age of reason."

In *The Reprieve*, the characters from the earlier book reappear along with some new ones; and we have seen how public figures, such as statesmen, have been included. The action covers the week (September 23–30, 1938) of the abject Chamberlain-Daladier kowtowing to Hitler's demands at Munich. Daniel and the pregnant Marcelle are honeymooning, as we have seen, in the Midi. Boris, thinking war will break out, enlists for three years in the army, an act he regrets when hostilities don't occur at that time. Similarly, Ivich, who has left Paris expecting to find war there, calls on Mathieu, who is about to leave for Nancy to go into the army; she gives him her virginity, an act she later regrets. Mathieu has been in Morocco with his brother and his sister-in-law Odette, with whom he nearly has a love affair. The night with Ivich is a compensation for his abstinence.

Among the new characters—and Chamberlain and other politicans sneeze or sign treaties among the experiences of the fictional people—one of the most important is the handsome young pacifist poet, Philippe, who doesn't really dare to be a pacifist. There are also the previously mentioned Czech, Milan Hlinka, and a number of others. The Communist Brunet hopes for war.

The Reprieve is a highly competent novel, though not a great one. Hence the technical tricks eventually become tiresome; such devices can be tolerated and even enjoyed in such a work as *Ulysses,* a book of comic gusto with important characters worth digging for; *The Reprieve* is merely a rather simple set of stories told with elaborate difficulty. Of course Sartre is trying to convey the confusion of the time, and the jangled lives of modern people, but perhaps these effects could have been suggested without making the reader's task so laborious. Actually, in relation to time, the novel merely copies other people's techniques rather than expressing Sartre's convictions on the subject, which leads him to diminish the importance of the past and to find that only the present and the future really exist, with the present existing solely in terms of the future. Such ideas become minimized when the main concentration is on the effect of simultanéisme. The philosophy of existentialisme is of course given rather full play, particularly in Mathieu's decision to commit himself. And the pressure of events upon all the characters intensifies the necessity for them to make some kind of choice. Within the great threatening beetletrap of the inevitable war, the possibilities of free action are minimized; yet there is still a certain area in which man can realize a degree of liberty.

The third volume, *Troubled Sleep*, begins by noting chronology in its chapter heads, then gets away from this practice. Simultanéisme plays little or almost no part in the technique of the book, which is, like much of the first volume, largely an episodic development of events in a third-person style. Sartre continues to show narrative skill, especially in his picture of the confusion of the French armies in time of defeat. And there are occasional fine passages, as when Gomez, away from painting for years, has a vision of color as he leaves a restaurant, of different colors flashing and swirling and pulsing on his eyes. And there is Daniel's view of occupied Paris, the Place de la Concorde (done long before André Malraux's garish, not altogether successful whitening up of the city in the 1960's) : a view of the grimy old Paris suggesting, here and there, the manner of the impressionistes:

> A moonlight quietude in the glare of the sun. Crude effigies of plaster in a circle about deserted spaces *will tell to generations yet unborn what men once were.* Sooty tears streaked the faces of tall pale ruins. . . . Stone, counterfeit stone made from the sugarloaves of history. . . . The desert stretched all about him: little flecks of sunlight from palace windows, tiny black and white objects, pigeons and numberless birds turned to stone because of feeding on statues. The only gay spot in this mineral landscape was the Nazi flag flying above the Hôtel de Crillon.

Troubled Sleep opens in New York, with the painter Gomez, who has previously been a minor character, taking a job which will entail popular presentations of art history. He has been a loyalist general in Spain, and is still shaking from the experience. On the day Paris falls he thinks the defeat is justified by France's failure to help Spain and Czechoslovakia. And then there is no more of Gomez, who has been used merely to set the stage in the steaming New York heat: the scene switches at once to his wife, Sarah, and their little boy, Pablo, in the throng of refugees going south from Paris. Meanwhile, in the city itself, Daniel, whose wife Marcelle is in the country, has an encounter with the young pacifist, Philippe, now a deserter. He is trying to kill himself, as Daniel had once tried to do. Daniel, attracted to him, involves himself in the young man's life and brings him home. The incident is skillfully written, with an important interplay of subtleties, but it is tame in comparison with Proust's description of the meeting of Jupien and the Baron de Charlus (in the *Cities of the Plain* section of *Remembrance of Things Past*), with its devoutly elaborate depravity intensified by the prevalent botanical symbolism. The scene in Sartre, although fine in itself, leads to nothing, at least in the material so far published, and the reader is left wondering what in the course of time happened to the relationship of Philippe and Daniel.

There are many other loose ends, though Mathieu is not one of them, at least not in this third volume. With a number of comrades in arms, he makes a last stand against the oncoming Germans, and is killed, or seems to be, in a belfry. Sartre the philosopher steps in at the last moment to point out Mathieu's "freedom." The world was being devoured by flames, and he kept firing away at a proud officer and at the street, the earth's beauty, the flowers and the gardens, indeed at all that he had loved: "He fired: he was cleansed, he was omnipotent, he was free"—and apparently dead. Satre, however, had an insert printed to say that Mathieu had actually not been killed.

In contrast, at the precise moment Mathieu appears to be killed, the Communist Brunet lets himself be captured. He determines to organize a Party cell among the other French prisoners, who at the end of the story are on a train being shipped to Germany. The two extracts of 1949 from the fourth volume show Brunet's experiences in the prison camp, including a futile attempt to escape; ironically, the Party has double-crossed Brunet by advocating submission, while he has been preaching resistance. There is a story to the effect that, in this fourth book, Sartre may have intended to show Daniel Sereno at last engaging in heroic action against the occupying Germans, and another to the effect that he was to become a collaborator and at

last succeed in killing himself in a greater self-disgust than
he had known before. Still another story suggests that
Mathieu was only wounded and would be resurrected.
Why Sartre never finished, or at least never published the
rest of this truncated tetralogy, one of the most ambitious
of all serious postwar ventures of its kind, remains a
puzzle so far. Philip Thody, in his book on Sartre in 1960,
said that "his failure to finish *The Roads to Freedom* may
be as much a result of his limitations as a writer as an
indication of his philosophical and political despair."
Simone de Beauvoir said in 1963 that Sartre didn't
complete his fourth volume because, while he was writing
it, the problems confronting the world had grown far
more complex than the simple situations of the time of
the war and the résistance. He didn't want to pitch his
story ten years ahead and put his people amid contemporary problems; he simply let the last volume slide away
from him. In her volume on Sartre (1953), the English
novelist and philosophy don, Iris Murdoch, had earlier
said that Sartre probably didn't finish the series because
he lacks the true novelist's sympathy with ordinary life.
He has in any event continued to present his ideas in
essays and in plays in which ideas dominate the action.

One of his most important postwar essays, in that it is
necessary for an understanding of much that occurs in the
later Sartre, is *Question de méthode* (1960; *Search for a
Method*), the introduction to the first of two volumes of
a longer work, *Critique de la raison dialectique* (*Critique
of Dialectical Reason*). This deals with social and political
questions largely neglected in *Being and Nothingness*. In
Search for a Method, Sartre comes out for Marxism as the
true dialectic of history as long as congregated mankind
depends so much upon material production and distribu-
tion. Man's freedom in these areas must be worked out,
Sartre says, before we can begin to talk about true
freedom. In making such statements, he is not necessarily
putting himself into the authoritarian camp, but rather
asserting a somewhat up-to-date version of the economic
view of history. He rejects the post-Marxist writers and,

frequently, the ostensible working out of Marxism in Soviet Russia. Yet it must be noted that, since Stalin's death, Sartre has (except for his criticism of the Budapest slaughters in 1956) been far more tolerant of pragmatic Communist activities. When the philosophy of Marxism takes in the existential, his book suggests, the existential itself will have no further reason for being: ingested into a larger philosophy, it will no longer be a specialized inquiry but rather the basis of all inquiry. Sartre's energies have lately been directed toward bringing about this condition.

His first postwar plays are *Morts sans sépulture* (1946; *Deaths Without Burial*, translated as *Men Without Shadows*) and *La Putain réspecteuse* (*The Respectful Prostitute*), produced together at the Théâtre Antoine. In *Deaths Without Burial*, Sartre wrote of the résistance, and of a number of maquis who fall into the hands of the Vichy milice. It is a play that should be revived periodically to remind everyone of what Pétain collaboration really meant. The résistance men are in the play tortured (onstage) and the women are raped (offstage). The irony of the situation is that the local leader, the secret of whose whereabouts the others are being tortured for, is arrested and brought in on a minor charge; but the others cannot betray Jean and he cannot give himself up because the lives of so many depend upon his safety. It is extreme application of existential theory, in this case the freedom to talk or not to under torture, which is itself a heightening of the anguish the existentialiste believes is at the base of life. The play, for all its melodrama—which includes a suicide and a murder and the eventual slaughter of all the prisoners—was philosophically heavy, with every idea embedded in the action exhaustively discussed.

The companion play, *The Respectful Prostitute*, is one of various indications of Sartre's anti-Americanism, though in all fairness it must be said that his picture of the Deep South and of American conformity is not greatly exaggerated. Not that the author's own France proved itself to be tolerant in regard to *La Putain réspecteuse*, in 1946, for at that time Madame Marthe

Richard was carrying on her campaign against filles de joie, or putains, and Sartre's play had to be advertised on the billboards of sophisticated Paris as *La* ▮▮▮▮ *réspecteuse*, as a result of which réspecteuse became a jesting synonym for a whore. The girl in the story was called respectful because, although a peddler of illicit relations, she believes solemnly in the smaller bourgeois moralities. Lizzie, a white prostitute who has come down from New York to set herself up in business, sees a white man murder a Negro, whose companion escapes. He comes to Lizzie secretly, and she promises that in court she will say that the rumor spread by the killer and his friends, that the two Negroes tried to rape her, is untrue. Yet she weakens (and makes possible the shooting of a second innocent Negro) when the uncle of the accused white man, a senator, calls on her and invokes Uncle Sam and the murderer's poor old mother: the dead Negro won't be missed, while the young white man is 100 per cent American, of an old family, a Harvard graduate, an officer ("we need officers"), the employer of two hundred men who would be out of work if he should be convicted, besides which he is a community leader and a bulwark against the Communists, the unions, and the Jews. There is caricature in this, conscious or not, for it is almost like a Soviet comedy about America in the Stalinist period, yet unfortunately it has much truth in it.

Sartre's next play was *Les Mains sales* (1948; *Dirty Hands*, translated as *Crime Passionnel* and as *Red Gloves*). It was first produced in Paris at the Antoine, with André Luguet in the role of Hoederer. The play is set in a supposedly eastern-European country called Illyria, but Hoerderer is no Orsino, and certainly no Malvolio. The drama is surrounded by a prologue and an epilogue. In the former, Hugo Barine, just out of jail after a two years' sentence for killing Hoerderer, head of the Communist underground during the German occupation, is trying to justify himself, but in telling his story, whose flashbacks make up the play, he is also examining himself. A bourgeois intellectual editing the Party's underground journal, Hugo is the kind of young man who would be chosen only in a roman policier to liquidate a Hoerderer. But in *Dirty Hands* he is fobbed off by the Party on Hoerderer as his secretary, and Hoerderer isn't fooled for a minute. The Party distrusts Hoerderer's policy, a united front of liberals and royalists against the Nazis. Hugo, as Hoerderer sees, is merely in revolt, an overgrown boy attacking his bourgeois background; but Hoerderer with his charm wins him over. When Hugo finds his wife Jessica in Hoerderer's arms, however, he at last carries out the Party's orders and kills him. But was he carrying out orders, or was the murder just a crime passionnel? In his self-examination as he tells the story, Hugo seems to exert his option of choice and apparently indicates that his act wasn't a crime passionnel, which would have been forgiven; so after a rather ambiguous statement, and saying that he isn't salvageable, he goes to meet his death at the hands of the Party's gunmen: for Hoerderer's policies have been approved since his own death, and he is now a Communist hero, whose ideas must not be questioned.

Communist criticisms of the play apparently made Sartre uncomfortable, and he objected to the American production of 1948 (featuring Charles Boyer, John Dall, and Joan Tetzel) because it used the title *Red Gloves*: the color had a sinister meaning. In any event, New York was one of the few places where the play failed. In 1954, Sartre was on hand in Vienna to express his antagonism against the local production, which he felt would increase the tension between East and West: he said he hadn't intended to attack communism but rather to dramatize the opposing views of two résistance groups. He further suggested that his feelings were no longer those of the time when he wrote the play—when, incidentally, he was publishing straightforward attacks on communism. It was difficult for many readers in the early 1960's to believe that a man of Sartre's evident intelligence could praise General Fidel Castro's reign of terror in Cuba, but he did.

Sartre had continued writing plays, for the most part

less forceful ones than his earlier attempts. *Le Diable et le bon Dieu* (1951; *The Devil and the Good God*, translated as *Lucifer and the Lord*), was Louis Jouvet's last production. Set in sixteenth-century Germany at the time of the peasants' revolt, the drama came from a suggestion of Jean-Louis Barrault, who told Sartre of an old Spanish play in which a gambler played at dice with good and evil as the stakes. Sartre saw existentialiste possibilities in this and eventually wrote a play which would have taken six hours on the stage. Jouvet cut out more than an hour, to Sartre's annoyance. That year of 1951 was also the year of Jean Cocteau's *Bacchus*, also about the Reformation period, and the two authors met to discuss their respective works and discovered with relief that they were not similar. Cocteau's play, however, caused an uproar and was denounced by François Mauriac and other spokesmen for religion. Audiences didn't cry out against Sartre's play, despite such lines as "Your Church is a putain," or at the hero Goetz's statement, when it is pointed out that he is a bastard: "Yes, like Jesus Christ." Some of the journalists, however, wrote severely about these matters, and the Church dutifully placed Sartre's writings on the Index. The actors, considering the play an "answer" to Paul Claudel's *Le Soulier de satin* (*The Satin Slipper*), used to say, "We are playing *Le Soulier de Satan*."

Lucifer and the Lord is a scattered and confused drama, partly held together by the personality of Goetz, the soldier of fortune, but as a character he too is scattered and confused. Goetz sacks Worms and kills crowds of people; later he gives his lands to the peasants, who then go to war. Goetz tries to do good, and is rarely successful. The English critic Philip Toynbee has remarked of the play, "As the most powerful military leader of his time and place there is no good reason for doubting (Goetz's) power to do evil, and Sartre, to elude this obvious difficulty, indulges in a typical piece of metaphysical sleight of hand." Sartre has tried to explain his concept of Goetz by saying that, as the illegitimate son of a nobleman and a peasant, he is rejected by both parties and has the problem of breaking "away from the anarchism of the right" so that he can take part in the peasants' revolt. But, Sartre says, he has tried to show that Goetz is destroying nothing when he thinks he is destroying most. In destroying human lives, he doesn't "disturb society or social judgments"; he is angered because all that he does benefits the rulers. His attempt to perform an act of absolute good in turning over his lands to the peasants also proves to be insignificant. "Whether he tries to arrive at the absolute through good or evil, he does nothing more than destroy human lives." But in trying to put all these concepts across dramatically, the author has created something of a philosophical hodgepodge, and at the last the play is, despite some impressive scenes, a huge, unclarified melodrama.

For Pierre Brasseur, who played Goetz with exuberance, Sartre adapted the old play of Alexandre Dumas père, *Kean*, based on the life of the English actor Edmund Kean, of whom Coleridge said, "Seeing him act was like reading Shakespeare by flashes of lightning." Sartre followed the main line of Dumas's play, but considerably improved many of its episodes and spruced up the dialogue. He was interested above all in the conflict between the imitative and the real, the man acting as an actor and the man acting as a man. Staged by Brasseur at the Sarah Bernhardt, the play was a popular success.

Sartre's one comedy, *Nekrassov* (1955), is an overextended satire (it plays for four hours) on the European brand of American-inspired anticommunism. A rogue named Georges de Valera, in order to dodge the police, fakes the identity of the Soviet minister of the interior, supposed to have fled from Russia. Taken up as a defector by the rightwing press, the pretended Nekrassov becomes a hero in Paris social circles, and at one fashionable reception gives a speech that is a pastiche of quotations from André Malraux. (It may be added that in this play Sartre also makes some jokes at his own expense.) When the real Nekrassov is reported as being seen publicly in Russia, de Valera gaily says that the Soviet government has pressed his double into service.

But when de Valera wants to be himself again, he

discovers that those who have been sponsoring him, including the French government, won't let him assume his own identity because he is too useful as the pseudo-Nekrassov. He sees that he has injured two leftwing reporters whom he has blithely said were in the pay of Moscow, so he squares matters by giving a leftwing paper an interview exposing his quackery. There is much in this that is amusing, and it is true that the American style of reaction is often foolish; the trouble with Sartre, however, as with many apologists for the left, is one-sidedness, like the anti-atom-bomb demonstrators in European capitals who shout their slogans and lift their signs in front of American embassies but not in front of Soviet headquarters. As Thody points out, Sartre has apparently not realized that NATO and the numerous American troops in Europe are not so much the cause of aggressive Russian policies as the result of them.

In 1960, Sartre was among the one hundred and twenty-one French intellectuals who signed a manifesto which said that French soldiers would be justified if they would refuse to serve in Algeria, that former colony which has since found it difficult to manage its own economy. In 1959, Sartre had brought out a play (at the Théâtre de la Renaissance) which had been inspired by the Algerian situation, although the scene was contemporary Germany: *Les Séquestres d'Altona* (*The Condemned of Altona*). In the household of the shipbuilder von Gerlach, at Altona, near Hamburg, the elder son has remained locked in his upstairs room during the thirteen years since he returned from the Russian front in 1946 with a dozen decorations. Seeming to be half-mad, he still wears his fading uniform. Various members of the family try to bring Franz back into the world, but only his father, soon doomed to die of cancer, knows Franz's secret. Franz had tortured Russian prisoners, though he tells his sister-in-law Johanna that he had refused to do so. During the long and complicated play, Franz's motive is made clear: in 1941 he had hidden a Polish rabbi in his room, but his father had arranged for the fugitive's arrest without implicating Franz. Years later Franz explains to his father that the rabbi's fate had demonstrated the horror of being powerless: Franz therefore accepted power as an officer of Hitler, and tortured enemy prisoners for information (as the French were reported doing at the time in Algeria). Both Franz and his father feel a weight of guilt, and they commit suicide together. This is Sartre's most pessimistic play, with the voluntary action of suicide as the answer to absurdity.

Jean-Paul Sarte wrote the preface to André Gorz's *Le Traître* (1958; *The Traitor*), which takes the form of an existential novel. It tells of the protagonist's childhood in Austria, and his flight with his mother at the time of the Anschluss: although reared as a Catholic, he had a Jewish father who was interned. As a boy, the protagonist is scorned at school as a Jew, yet on the streets he feels the magnetism of Nazi parades. In Switzerland he grows up struggling with the problems of modern man without solving them, without establishing an identity. After the war he meets Morel (Sartre), and their discussions awaken the rootless exile who has refused to consider action and involvement. Evading Morel's challenge that he become "engaged" in affirmative activity, the protagonist tries to escape by working in the mines in the Congo, but he eventually feels the pull of Paris and becomes an existentialist there. Gorz in recounting these adventures discovers four stages in life's journey: "We," "They," "You," and the final liberation of "I," the recognition of the free self. En route to his goal he examines Marxism and psychoanalysis and explains his personal relationships, not only with Morel but with the two women in his life, given the fictional names of Kay and L. Sartre in his preface says that the author, living in Paris, maintains an outward responsibility in a conventional job. But the story deals with his inward life: in his own terms he is a "traitor," indulging in ambiguity. Yet at the same time he is "betrayed" because he had taken a position; the book ends with him hoping "for something better." This récit (story, narrative, report) is, like so much writing in recent France, a true story presented in imaginative guise.

As for the acknowledged leader of the existentialistes,

he has been dealt with sensibly by the English novelist and critic, Rayner Heppenstall, who says perceptively in *The Fourfold Tradition* (1961) that it may be too early to write off Sartre as a spent force, for although he certainly was a force, he has "tired us out. Nobody with a quiet and continuing interest in literature wants to think about him any longer." But he will be thought of again, Heppenstall points out in this book which deftly shows the interaction of French and British literature: "Even if [Sartre] never writes another word worth reading, his literary career of fifteen years was productive of one or two fine works and a plenitude of ideas, some of which are still new." Interestingly, Sartre rejected the Nobel Prize in 1964, the year in which he brought out *Les Mots* (*The Words*), the brilliant autobiography of a part of his childhood.

3 *Simone de Beauvoir*

One of the most interesting associations of Sartreisme—who indeed may have to some extent helped create the latter—is Simone de Beauvoir, who was born in 1908, five years after Sartre. In one of her memoirs she says she was born in a room looking down the Boulevard Raspail: actually, this was over the Café de la Rotonde, where in the early 1900's those exiles Lenin and Trotsky used to play chess, and where in the 1920's the Hemingway set often gathered. It is the heart of Montparnasse. Mlle. de Beauvoir attended the nearby Sorbonne, where she became the friend of Sartre. After taking her degree in philosophy in 1929, she taught at various places in the provinces and in Paris, until in 1943 she decided to devote her working hours to writing. Her contribution to French existentialiste thinking has been major. In the years just after the war, she and Sartre made the cafés of the place Saint Germain-des-Prés famous as existentialiste meeting places: les Deux Magots, le Café Flore, and la Brasserie Lipp.

Simone de Beauvoir's first novel was *l'Invitée* (1943;

The Invited Guest, translated as *She Came to Stay*). The guest is Xavière, a girl from the provinces who is invited to live with Pierre, a theatrical producer, and his mistress Françoise. Xavière, who has long blonde hair like Ivich in Sartre's *The Roads to Freedom*, one night at a café burns her hand with a match, recalling Ivich's deliberate cutting of her own hand in the first volume of Sartre's series. The epigraph for *She Came to Stay* is a sentence from Hegel which Sartre had previously quoted emphatically: "Each consciousness seeks the death of the other." Xavière becomes "the other" in the relationship between Françoise and Pierre. The novel—which is among other things a complicated examination of the sadism and masochism which, like Freud, the existentialists find in most love relationships—shows Pierre becoming attracted to Xavière, whom Françoise tries to instruct as if she were a pupil. Xavière introduces another element by having an affair with an actor with whom Françoise is also involved. Pierre and Françoise, who have long lived together in a kind of existentialiste freedom, conventional though their relationship is, are changed by the dominating influence of the inexperienced young girl. When Pierre goes off to war, Françoise attempts once again to be her friend. But she discovers that Xavière thinks of her as the ordinarily jealous woman, living in what the existentialists would regard as mauvaise foi, or bad faith. This is true enough, but Françoise doesn't recognize it. She sees Xavière as "the other," and exercises her existential choice of action by turning on the gas in the sleeping girl's bedroom so that her resultant death looks like suicide.

In her next novel, *Le Sang des autres* (1944; *The Blood of Others*), Simone de Beauvoir portrays Jean Blomart, a young bourgeois intellectual who in the 1930's decides to take the side of the working classes. He also decides to have nothing to do with Hélène, the fiancée of a friend of Jean's. Hélène is a shallow girl, but in the course of the novel Jean falls in love with her. After she has for a while accepted the occupation, and Nazi propaganda, Hélène turns against such ideas and joins Jean in the résistance.

As one of its leaders, Jean has a fairly safe, behind-the-lines station. Hélène, in the forefront of an action, is fatally wounded. She dies in Jean's arms, with words of love. All human beings are responsible for "the blood of others." Jean feels that freedom is the element that saves every man from himself and others. With Hélène just dead, Jean leads the maquis into attack. Whatever the philosophical implications of the novel, it is a vivid story and a notable picture of its time, with credible characters: the change in Hélène, for example, is convincingly presented. This is not only one of the best, but one of the few good surviving novels, of wartime France.

Mlle. de Beauvoir's play, *Les Bouches inutiles* (1945; *Useless Mouths*) deals with the "extreme situation" through which existential writers examine man's behavior: it concerns a besieged town in Flanders in which the question comes up as to whether the women and children should still be fed: do we have the right to sacrifice individuals for a general good in the future? The author, who believed that the dialogue in *She Came to Stay* indicated that she could write for the stage, said later that she felt she had moralized too much in *Useless Mouths*. Her next novel, *Tous les Hommes sont mortels* (1947; *All Men Are Mortal*), examined the idea of immortality: a man in thirteenth-century Italy drinks, out of choice, a potion that will make him immortal. But as the centuries pass, those he knows dies, and his projects fade away; by the nineteenth century he often goes into cataleptic trances he has learned how to induce. The story stresses the responsibility to, and the relationship with, others; and it shows that prolonged human life would be meaningless in that the immortal man would always see the gradual destruction of his enterprises.

Simone de Beauvoir also wrote a number of existentialiste essays, including *Pour une Morale de l'ambiguïté* (1947; *The Ethics of Ambiguity*), which advocates the need for pointing out to those who have chosen bad faith that other possibilities of conduct are open to them. Her popular volume, *Le Deuxième Sexe* (1949; *The*

Second Sex), is staunch feminist doctrine. In it she shows how most women have to live in various manifestations of bad faith because the man's world is forced upon them. This book, however, is more than a strident thesis, for its investigation of the development of woman, spiritually and erotically, is thorough and seasoned. The main points of the book are that women are not at all inferior to men, and that they must realize themselves through free action. A year before this volume appeared, Mlle. de Beauvoir had written a detailed and rather crabby (however true in parts) volume about the United States, *l'Amérique le jour au jour* (1948; *America Day by Day*). Some years later, however, she could find much to praise in a society in which men couldn't under any terms realize freedom of action: *La Longue Marche* (1957; *The Long March*), an essay, too-little critical, on Communist China. Sure, America has its faults, and some of them are serious ones. As to Communist China, the question might be asked, "But have you *been* there?"—yet a great many people didn't have to go to Nazi Germany to know what, in spite of all the pro-Hitler propaganda, the place was like (Belsen and Buchenwald).

Simone de Beauvoir's best-known novel, *Les Mandarins* (1954; *The Mandarins*), won the Goncourt Prize. The story is partly an autobiography, and recognizable portraits of leading members of the existentialiste movement and of other postwar French literary figures occur throughout the book: Sartre, Camus, Raymond Aron, and others. During two visits to America, the heroine—who is a psychiatrist—has a love affair with an American writer, portrayed in this book as Lewis Brogan, somewhat on the wild side.

Anne Debreuilh, whose husband Robert is nothing else than a famous Sartre-like philosophy professor at the Sorbonne, feels at thirty-nine that she is aging and, throughout the book, she behaves with a certain desperation. Anne's story is counterpointed with that of her husband's Camus-like friend Henri (who will eventually marry Anne's neurotic daughter) and of Henri's mistress,

Paula. Once when Paula has planned to kill herself, she lets Anne take a vial of poison away from her. Anne, instead of disposing of it, leaves it in her own drawer, and after Lewis Brogan has in effect cast her off, she is tempted to use it, but doesn't. She has realized that, however imperfect her relationship with Robert may have been at times, he has given her twenty years of companionship without destroying her solitude. At the end of the book, she reflects: "My death doesn't belong to me. The vial is still here, where my hand can reach it; death is still here. But the living are present even more. At least as long as Robert lives, I won't be able to escape them. I put away the vial. Condemned to death; but also condemned to live! . . . Perhaps some day I'll be happy again. Who knows?"

It's a patterned existentialiste ending. The book itself is too long, too talky, but there are many effective passages, particularly the descriptions of Anne's experiences in Chicago, New York, and a Mexican town. The introduction of modern French politics into the story isn't intrusive since it is made an organic part of the lives of the characters involved, and the book dramatizes the quarrel of 1952, essentially political, between Camus and Sartre. Yet *The Mandarins* doesn't stand out emphatically as a French novel of the first importance. It is an interesting picture of the France after the war, and often an interesting picture of a woman.

A more interesting picture of a woman's life occurs in Simone de Beauvoir's autobiographical volumes, *Mémoires d'une fille rangée* (1958; *Memoirs of a Dutiful Daughter*) and *La Force de l'âge* (1960; *The Prime of Life*); her own celebrated beauty adds piquancy to the narratives. The first of these volumes tells more graphically than perhaps it has ever been told before what it is like to be a growing girl. It is certainly one of the most expert and absorbing confessionals ever written by a woman. It has been mentioned that Simone de Beauvoir was born above the Café de la Rotonde; she was the daughter of a Catholic lawyer of severely conservative outlook. Yet here was early childhood among the cafés of Montparnasse. The book contains some fine portraits: her parents and various relatives, including the cousin Jacques, with whom she fell in love, and who turned out to be a derelict, as well as her lively friend Zaza, who in the fullness of youth died suddenly. In the last parts of the book, Mlle. de Beauvoir is a student, meeting Sartre and others. But the most remarkable passages in it are those concerned with the turbulence of adolescence: these are frank, female, and French. In *The Prime of Life*, the author covers the years from 1929 to the eve of the liberation of Paris in 1944, and excitingly tells of her years as a teacher and writer, of the development of the French existentialiste movement, and of the résistance. In *La Force des choses* (1963; *Force of Circumstance*), Mlle. de Beauvoir brought her autobiography up into the 1960's, in a volume that had less inward quality than its two predecessors. In it she reveals herself as caught up in historic events too recent to warrant extended treatment here: the confusion of postwar France, above all in the thorny Indochina and Algeria situations. As usual, she is critical of the United States, often plausibly, though her censure would be more forceful if she didn't so uncritically accept Red China, Soviet Russia, and Castro's Cuba.

Simone de Beauvoir is a reputable writer of philosophical essays and a fine novelist; she is, except for her frequent political blindness, a supreme autobiographer. In 1963, she published a long essay on the Marquis de Sade, accompanied by selections from his writings. She doesn't overpraise his work, but sees him as an important figure: though unaware of action in the existential sense, he was certainly not unaware of suffering. He was aware of the brutality of existence, and the hypocrisy by whose means most people live through it: "He surpassed the sensualism of his age to transform it into an ethic of authenticity."

4 *The Later Career of Camus*

The early life of Albert Camus, from his birth in Algeria through his work in France for the wartime résistance, culminated in his first novel, *l'Étranger* (1942; *The Stranger*) and his first play to be produced in Paris, *Le Malentendu* (1943; *The Misunderstanding*), as well as in his essays, *Le Mythe de Sisyphe* (1943; *The Myth of Sisyphus*) and *Lettres à un ami allemand* (1945; *Letters to a German Friend*). As existentialisme developed as a French school, Camus became associated with it, and though he often violently disclaimed connection with it, he is still generally regarded as an existentialiste. It might be more proper to place him in the school of the absurd, since absurdity was from the first one of the principal concepts in his work. Yet this is also to some extent an existential concept. Ultimately, the slight difference in classification may not matter greatly. In 1962, two years after Camus's death, Thomas Hanna, who had earlier written *The Thought and Art of Albert Camus*, discussed him again in *The Lyric Existentialists*, among whom he also placed Kierkegaard and Nietzsche.

Camus's idea of absurdity is outlined in his *Sisyphus* book, in which the mythological figure who gives it its name is shown as the absurd creature pushing a stone uphill, a stone which grows larger the farther up it goes, until finally it eludes him and bounces back downhill, after which he starts over again in his eternal, futile activity. And yet he is happy in this absurdity, as man is happy to go through the absurdity of daily living rather than seeking death, when in a universe so ridiculous the most sensible action would seem to be committing suicide. But man continually combats nihilism.

The play *Caligula*, whose earlier version Camus had written in Algiers in the late 1930's, came out at the Théâtre Hébertot in September, 1945, a month after the Germans had been driven from Paris. Gérard Philipe scored a great success as Caligula in the drama, which has often been revived, before and after Philipe's death. To its first audiences, the play's lustful cruelty was reminiscent of the Nazis—Hitler still had some eight months left—but Camus had drawn heavily upon the ancient Roman chronicler Suetonius. Of course he filled the play with his own attitudes toward absurdity: Caligula, in love with his sister Drusilla and living with her as his wife, disappears for three days after her unexpected death. He has in the past been a benevolent young emperor, but now he feels the absurdity of life, which he emphasizes by weird masquerades, by deliberately causing famine, and by murdering his subjects. All this is illogical, yet it contains a furious logic; and it all ends when Caligula himself is murdered.

After *Caligula*, Camus wrote two more original plays which were produced: *l'État de siège* (1946; *The State of Siege*) and *Les Justes* (1949; *The Just*, translated as *The Just Assassins*). After this he brought out four adaptations: *Les Ésprits* (1953; *The Spirits*, after Pierre de Larivey), *La Dévotion à la croix* (1953; *Devotion to the Cross*, after Pedro Calderón de la Barca), *Un Cas intéressant* (1955; *An Interesting Case*, after Dino Buzzati), *Requiem pour une nonne* (1956; *Requiem for a Nun*, after William Faulkner), and *Les Possédés* (1959; *The Possessed*, after Fyodor Dostoevsky). The first three of these were merely by-products, jeux d'esprit, theatrical carpentry, but Camus took the last two seriously. In the preface to the published edition of *The Possessed*, Camus said that he had always regarded Dostoevsky's novel among the handful of works he regarded above all others, and that he had dreamed for some twenty years of dramatizing it. Camus notes that one of the story's two principal plots concerns a political assassination, hence it has present-day application. In his program note to the adaptation, of Faulkner, Camus said he was interested in two aspects of the theater: technical problems and the projection of tragedy in modern terms. Faulkner's *Requiem* is a series of loose dialogues which Camus tightened and presented in a language not strictly colloquial and yet not so literary that it sounds unreal on the stage. The Temple Drake side of the story, as Camus treats it, seems too trivial to be really tragic; Camus instead attempts to put the tragic elements of the play into the experience of the Negro woman, Nancy Mannigoe.

Camus's two last original plays were *l'État de siège* (1948; *The State of Siege*) and *Les Justes* (1950; *The Just*), the latter dealing with Russian revolutionaries in 1905. (Camus was supposedly working on a Don Juan drama at the time of his death.) *The State of Siege* at the Marigny in October, 1948 featured Jean-Louis Barrault and his wife, Madeleine Renault, as well as Pierre Brasseur, Pierre Bertin, and Maria Casarès. The music was by Oscar Honegger. The play has correspondences with the novel, set in North Africa, which Camus had brought out the year before: *La Peste* (*The Plague*).

Camus in his preface to the published version of the play explained that, as early as 1941, Barrault had been interested in creating a dramatic spectacle around the "myth" of the plague as it had been discussed by Antonin Artaud (1896–1948), the surréalise poet who became a theatrical theorist and finally sank into occultism and madness. The original idea was to build a story around Daniel Defoe's *A Journal of the Plague Year*; when Barrault discussed the matter with Camus after the latter had published his novel, *The Plague* (which had in its turn drawn upon Defoe), a new concept was evoked, "a myth which could be comprehended by all audiences in 1948." Hence the poetic-philosophical spectacle whose result was what Camus called a hymn to the only religion still alive: freedom.

On the stage, the plague is personified by a uniformed figure which, as played by Pierre Bertin with rimless glasses, looked like Heinrich Himmler. This creature dominates Cádiz until Diego (played by Barrault) leads the citizens in a successful revolt against him. When presented at the Marigny, *The State of Siege* was a fiasco. Barrault says in one of his theater essays that some members of the audience on the first night were pleased at the failure, which to him was a physical pain, a wound that still rankled in him years later. Part of the fault may have been in Barrault's loose-rhythmed style of production, but the play itself, despite some effective choruses, was an uneasy compromise between poetic symbolism and prosaic topical references. And, for all the horror and terror of their situation, the characters were too generalized to engage the empathy of the audience. Throughout, what should be concrete is too abstract.

Camus's *The Just*, with Serge Reggiani and Maria Casarès, was decidedly more successful at the Hébertot in December, 1959. This is the story of the assassination, in Russia in 1905, of a grand duke. Based on history and memiors, the drama nevertheless works out several Camusian themes, particularly in showing the terrorists as divided between hatred of their aristocratic oppressors and the idealism of their cause. The student, Ivan (Yanek) Kaliayev, who is an idealist, is unable to throw the bomb into the grand duke's carriage on his first opportunity because there are children in it. Ivan's associate Stepan takes him to task for his failure, one of the points of the play which is unhistorical since the revolutionaries didn't want the children murdered. But Stepan scolds Yanek for weakness. Later, Yanek finds the grand duke alone in the carriage and succeeds in killing him.

Imprisoned, Yanek is visited by a sly police investigator and by the grand duchess, who has become slightly unbalanced since her husband's assassination; she begs Yanek to turn to the church. Yanek refuses to accept guilt, for he has killed an idea, not a man, and he has acted out of love, love of humanity. In a final act, the terrorists who remain uncaught are together on the night of Yanek's execution, debating the validity of their deed. The strong-minded Dora asserts her willingness to be the next one to throw a bomb, yet her conscience disturbs her: "It is so much easier to die of contradictions than to live with them."

Like all Camus's work for the theater, this play is too

didactic, but it has a fine dramatic tension, particularly when Ivan prepares to go out and commit the assassination. Camus in a program note emphasized the didactic tone of the play when he wrote that those living in the middle of the twentieth century could learn a moral lesson from the selfless revolutionaries of 1905: today's revolutionaries are brutal and immoral in their efforts to set up a classless society.

For all his experience in the theater, dating from his early youth, Camus was perhaps better equipped to be a writer of fiction and essays than of plays. His novel of 1947, *The Plague*, has been mentioned as having a North African setting. Specifically this is Oran, in Algeria, where suddenly the rats begin to die with bloody mouths. Soon people start to die, too, though the medical profession is cautiously slow in designating an epidemic. Then it is upon them, and the city is cut off from the world. The principal figure in the novel is Dr. Bernard Rieux, who devotes himself to fighting the plague. His wife, who is ill, has left before the epidemic began, and she dies while away. The Parisian journalist, Raymond Rambert, arranges to have some Spanish smugglers assist him to escape, but he finally decides to stay and help fight the plague. Jean Tarrou works with Rieux to form a group of volunteers, and Rambert joins them. Tarrou, who with Father Paneloux will die in the plague, had left home in his youth because he was horrified that his father, as prosecutor, had to send people to death. But in his activity as a political agitator he has discovered that he too is in effect an executioner. He finds that helping to organize the sanitary corp is meaningful. For him the plague provides the crisis which usually heightens the action of existentialist writings: the crisis makes one start again, not from the potential but from the actual. He is even capable of cheering up the criminal, Cottard, who had tried to hang himself but had been cut down. Tarrou assures Cottard that the police will not come after him now because of the plague: no one ever has two diseases at the same time, for if you have cancer or galloping consumption you don't get the plague, which itself has stopped police activity. "We have police these days; no past or present crimes or criminals—only condemned men living in hope of the most capricious of pardons; and among them are the police themselves."

The philosophical underlining of the story isn't sufficiently heavy to spoil it, nor is its symbolism, though easy to see, intrusive. To most Frenchmen of the time, the plague was the Nazi occupation as they remembered it; Camus, of course, had a larger intention, which included all calamities on the order of Nazism. But the story told is effective because it remains grounded in reality: even, with the descriptions of rats, sickness, and death, in a kind of naturalism. The people and their problems are believable, though after the plague stops with the coming of cold weather, life remains the absurd and puzzling thing it was before. Rieux sees that he has no more actual knowledge of plague than he had previously. But he has acted, and continued to act, in the face of the inexplicable.

Some of Camus's essays, such as *The Myth of Sisyphus*, are so closely related to his imaginative work as to be virtually a part of it. This distinctly applies to *l'Homme revolté* (1951; *The Rebelling Man*, translated as *The Rebel: An Essay on Man in Revolt*). This is an examination of modern revolutions, that is those since 1789, all of which Camus finds leading to authoritarianism. Camus opposes what he calls the German and the historical, which he often identifies with the Marxist. L'esprit Méditerranéen—the Mediterranean spirit of modern French, Spanish, and Italian thinkers, deriving from ancient Greece—went down to defeat in the nineteenth century under the hammerings of Hegel and Nietzsche, of Marx and Engels. Yet Camus is on the side of les meurtriers délicats (the fastidious assassins), of whom he wrote in *The Just*—the terrorists of 1905, who were not trying to destroy men but ideas. (Yanek said, "It is not a man I am killing; I am killing despotism.") What Camus calls the Caesarian revolution is, however, another matter, for it uses its police, its trials, and its excommunications in an effort to disprove and deny human nature. It is against this that man must be in rebellion.

In *Sisyphus*, Sartre had, after revealing the absurdity of the world, questioned whether or not suicide wasn't the sensible response, and had decided that suicide gave too much importance to death—life itself is the only certainty. L'homme absurde, the absurd man, challenges death and nihilism with every instant of his life. In *The Rebel*, Camus points out that the important question is one of enduring: in deciding to live, we do so because our life has some value, but if we decide to rebel we do this because society has values. These are difficult to discover but, when found, they will embody the necessity of rebelling on behalf of the unity that freedom brings: "The rebel without doubt demands a certain freedom for himself; but not in any case, if he is consistent, does he demand the destruction of the life or liberty of anyone else. He degrades no one. The freedom he asks for he claims for everyone; what he refuses he forbids to everyone. He is not just a slave against a master, but rather a man against the world of master and slave."

The significant battle of our time, Camus says, is not so much between German historical ideology and Christian political thinking, which often resemble one another, as between "the German dreams and the Mediterranean tradition, between the violence of eternal adolescence and mature strength, between nostalgia heightened by knowledge as well as books and courage tempered and clarified by the experience of life; in short, history against nature." The "strange joy that helps one to live and die" is now born, and the time has come to forsake the "adolescent furies" of this epoch. It is time to "reshape the spirit of our age."

With much of this, the type of thinking that is now called liberal in America and England would be in harmony. The American extreme right wing, too unintelligent to understand it, and in any event (whether or not consciously so) sympathetic to the Teutonic form of totalitarianism, wouldn't and hasn't found much to agree

with in these words of Camus; but such people are
illiterate anyhow. The British right wing, openly Fascist
in opposition to the liberalism found in the Labour and
Conservative Party majorities, understands part of Camus's
argument, dialectically, and would reject it. Unfortunately, the right wing in France, the heirs of the anti-
Dreyfusards, made Camus into a kind of darling after *The
Rebel*, and even his expressed atheism didn't alienate him
from many clerical reactionaries. He wasn't expressing the
views of these groups, but of genuine liberals anywhere;
unfortunately France, despite her confusion of multiple
political parties, allows little space for a reasonable liberalism. Indeed, the intellectual left, particularly Sartre,
attacked Camus after *The Rebel*, and Camus answered,
creating one of the liveliest postwar literary quarrels, but
one that didn't particularly resolve the confusions in the
arguments of either side. Sartre felt that Camus didn't
give enough weight to political action, and Camus felt
that Sartre gave too much emphasis to it. Basically, both
believed in the absurd, but Camus in his later writing was
advocating moderation, a kind of nonaction, and pointed
out that, as an existentialiste, which Camus emphatically
declared he himself was not, Sartre was entangling himself
in a contradiction by mixing a deterministic philosophy
such as Marxism with existentialisme, a philosophy which
claimed to lead to freedom through good action (and the
goodness of action was relative in the deterministic
philosophy, which is any event precluded free action).
Sartre at one point was so irritated that he abandoned all
ad rem positions and said that Camus had left himself
nowhere to go except the Galápagos Islands. Significantly
enough, the other great explosion besides Marxism in
nineteenth-century thought was stimulated by the voyage
made to the Galápagos by Charles Darwin.

Many of Camus's journalistic articles were collected in
the volumes *Actuelles, I, II, III* (a selection of these
essays was published in English in 1961 as *Resistance,
Rebellion, and Death*). They show that, although he
refused to see man as primarily political, Camus was

deeply aware of the importance of politics. He regarded it
as separated from ethics, and he was opposed to all forms
of violent repression; he attacked both Franco's Spain and
Stalin's Russia. He opposed the admission of Spain to
UNESCO, and during the Algerian crisis, when so many
French intellectuals wanted Algeria "freed," since reten-
tion of it meant colonialism, Camus wanted France and
Algeria to work out a union, the lack of which, as we now
see, has led to a somewhat impoverished Algeria, whose
inhabitants don't have the technical skill of their French
predecessors—a country which may have to come under
the "protection" of Soviet Russia. Camus, opposed to
tyranny, racism, monopoly, and rigid state control, was an
intellectual of the left—a difficult rôle in France, particularly when Sartre was sniping at his former associate on
Combat, attacking him for lack of commitment, which
really meant aloofness from Party politics. But Camus
opposed fanatical political extremes, whether of the type
that wears the screaming face of a Hitler or the smooth
mask of a Stalin.

The last major work by Camus was the short novel, *La
Chute* (1956; *The Fall*), which will be discussed after his
collection of six stories, *l'Exile et le royaume* (1957; *Exile
and the Kingdom*). In that same year of 1957, Camus was
given the Nobel Prize, and in Stockholm in December he
made a characteristic speech (*Discourse de Suède*, 1958;
Swedish Discourse) saying that the artist today cannot
serve "those who make history," but rather those who are
subject to it. He spoke of himself and others who, in the
preceding two decades, had suffered from "utterly insane
history," during which time he felt that it was an honor to
be a writer because writing obligated a man to do more
than write. Many of his generation had succumbed to
despair and nihilism, but most Frenchmen and other
Europeans had fought against such ideas in order to
"discover some kind of legitimacy." And now the task is
to keep the whole world from self-destruction. The writer
should not become "a preacher of virtue," though Camus
admitted that he had never forgotten the sunlight, the joy

of life, and the sense of freedom of his early years. This nostalgia might account for many of his mistakes, his failures, but those early memories "undoubtedly helped me to understand my calling," and they still help him to remain implicitly on the side of "the many silent men who, all over the world, endure the life that has been made for them only because they remember or briefly live again through free moments of happiness."

In 1957, the year of the Nobel Prize and of his speech referring to the sunlight of his early life, Camus reissued the volume of essays he had written in Algeria and published in 1937: *l'Envers et l'endroit* (*The Wrong Side and the Right Side*), mentioned earlier as one of the first expressions of the author's irony and pessimism. Yet, even if the world of this book has no comfort for man, that world is still beautiful. In the preface to the 1957 reprint, Camus said that his early poverty in Algeria was not a misfortune, "for the richness of light there compensated for it. Even my rebellions were brightened by this light. They were almost always, I think I can say without cheating, rebellions for everyone, and for the purpose of raising everyone's life into this light." He spoke of literary circles in Paris, and of how, to escape their dangerous influence, he had developed a surly manner. Yet he feels that his world is still what it was at the time of the early book, which is to say that his early world is "that old woman, a silent mother, poverty, the light on the olive trees of Italy, solitary and collective love, all that are witnesses, in my eyes, of truth." He states that, "like everyone else, somehow or other, I tried to realize myself through an ethic. It is this, alas, which has cost me most."

The short stories and novellas which appeared in 1957 in *Exile and the Kingdom* attracted little attention in comparison with Camus's other work, probably because they offer meager ground for controversy. The single exception might be "Le Renégat" ("The Renegade"), a stream-of-consciousness story about a priest who, tortured and mutilated by savages in Africa, becomes an ardent worshiper of their idol. The other stories, however brilliantly done, threaten to provoke little of the controversy inherent in the theme of "The Renegade." The tale called "La Femme adultère" ("The Adulterous Woman") is a somewhat D. H. Lawrence-like story of a Frenchwoman who accompanies her husband on a business trip to North Africa and, falling in love with the setting, goes out at night to "give herself" to it. "Les Muets" ("The Silent Men"), also set in North Africa, is a severely plain story of a group of laborers who will not speak to their employer, a shopowner, because they have lost a strike and then, when his little daughter is taken ill, find that out of shyness they cannot speak to him. "L'Hôte" ("The Guest") is the story of a French schoolmaster in Algeria upon whom the police force an Arab prisoner, telling him that he must escort the man fifteen miles to the next police station; Daru tries to help the prisoner escape, but the Arab doesn't understand and remains in captivity, after which Daru finds that the prisoner's friends have written on the school blackboard: "You turned in our brother. You will pay for this," and then the author ends the story with the comment about Daru, "In this enormous landscape which he had loved so much, he was alone." In "Jonas, ou l'artiste au travail" ("The Artist at Work"), Camus presented a humorous story, reminiscent of situations in Henry James in which the artist who has become famous has difficulty in finding his necessary solitude. "La Pierre qui pousse" ("The Growing Stone") is the ironic story of an engineer in Brazil who achieves friendship by carrying on his head for a long distance the heavy stone another man had vowed to Christ to carry on the next saint's day: the engineer, overcoming his loneliness by gaining a friend, and the goodwill of the friend's family, is at one level another vision of the Sisyphus myth, this time with an apparently absurd action leading to a definite good.

In his last novel, *The Fall*, Camus left the bright warmth of the southlands for a shabby waterfront bar in Amsterdam, and the rainy streets of that northern city, and even the Zuider Zee. The book, the kind of short

novel the French call a récit, is a monologue delivered to a
visiting French lawyer, sparsely characterized, across five
afternoons and nights. The ancient mariner who has fixed
upon the visitor is also a lawyer, formerly a successful one
in Paris, who is now lacerated by guilt, but a guilt he feels
all men share. His very name, Jean-Baptiste Clamence,
emphasizes the symbolic title of the book, La Chute, or
The Fall, with its suggestion of John the Baptist and, in
the surname, a punning combination of the words for
crying out and for mercy. Interestingly, after the French
reviews of the book, some of which intimated that
Camus's theological implications were in contrast with
everything in his earlier work and that they perhaps
heralded a religious conversion, Camus put at the head of
the English translation of his novel part of the preface
Mikhail Lermontov had used, more than a century before,
for one of the later editions of his novel A Hero of Our
Time: "Some were grievously insulted at being given as a
model such an immortal fellow as a Hero of Our Time;
others shrewdly suggested that the author had pictured
himself and his acquaintances. . . . A Hero of Our Time,
gentleman, is in actuality a portrait, but not of an individual man; it is a portrait fully concentrating the vices of
our whole generation." Camus told an interviewer in 1956
that what he was particularly aiming at in The Fall was
writers who try to bring members of the bourgeois group
into communism by making them feel that they share
in the evils of their society; as Thody remarks, "far from
seriously expressing a belief in universal human wickedness
in La Chute, Camus is satirizing and attacking it. He sees
it as a weapon for enslaving men, in the same way as, in
l'Homme revolté, he showed that nihilism and the Hege-
lian theory of history could be used for the same purpose.
In the prière d'insérer (request to publish)—the little
explanatory note that French authors sometimes slip into
their books—Camus remarked that Clamence 'has a
modern heart, that is to say that he cannot bear to be
judged. He thus hastens to accuse himself, but it is so
that he may more easily judge other people.' "
In his Paris career, Clamence had been so successful

that he could afford to take as clients many of the downtrodden, whom he defended for justice' sake and, partly, out of his dislike for judges. He was a master of living: "My harmony with life was complete, I adhered to it at every level, refused none of its irony, its grandeur, nor its demands." He is often epigrammatic, with a pungent humor, as when he tells his listener that many of the murderers whose cases he accepted had been stimulated by the possibility of fame: "To get notoriety, one merely has to kill one's concierge. In most cases this unfortunately produces only a momentary reputation, since there are so many concierges who deserve to have their throats cut. And so many who get what they deserve." Or: "You see, a person of my acquaintance used to divide human beings into three categories: those who prefer to have nothing to hide rather than be obliged to lie, those who prefer to lie rather than have nothing to hide, and finally those who at the same time like both lies and secrecy."

What is behind these astringent aphorisms?—a man who had hated judges and has become what he calls a juge-pénitent (judge-penitent), telling his story to strangers. The high point of his story is that one night as he was crossing the Pont-Royal over the Seine he had seen a young woman on the bridge and, a moment later, heard her body fall as she leaped into the river, and then, with her cries for help jangling in his ears he had paused a moment but had gone on. A few years later he had the idea that laughter kept following him, and he began to deteriorate: he felt that he had performed his good deeds for applause and fame, for when no one was near he refused to help another human being, had merely "passed by on the other side," a point he has in common with many of today's city-dwellers who refrain from going to help those attacked on the streets.

The "fall" of Clamence is gradual: "How can I tell you? Things slipped. Yes, everything slipped away from me." Clamence sank into debauchery and lost his career and his friends. The friends began sliding away when they discovered that Clamence had in effect become a judge, was judging them along with the rest of mankind. As he ends his elongated monologue, Jean-Baptiste Clamence apostrophizes the unknown young woman to jump into the water again so that he might have a second chance of saving both of them: "A second chance, what a dangerous idea! . . . We'd have to go through with it. Brr . . . ! The water's too cold! But let's not worry! It's too late now. It will always be too late. Fortunately!" And so the book ends.

Clamence had learned, he says, "on the bridges of Paris," that what he was really afraid of was freedom. "So, long live the master, whoever he is, who will replace the laws of heaven." Besides, freedom is ultimately a court sentence, "too heavy to bear, particularly when you're sick with fever, or miserable, or love no one." Yet Clamence despite his hailing of "the master"—which like much of his utterance is ironic—doesn't want a police state. He says bitterly that Europe has become lucid, having replaced dialogue with the communiqué. " 'Here is the truth,' we say. 'We can talk about it if you want; we aren't interested. But in a few more years the police will show you that I'm right.' " Camus also takes a few cuts at some of his Parisian opponents, as when he speaks of the childishness of "the café atheists."

Not attempting to rescue the young woman who had leaped into the Seine isn't Clamence's only act of nonparticipation. Mobilized in the war, he saw no action other than the retreat, and after being demobilized inquired about joining the résistance; but after he learned how to become part of it, he didn't (unlike Camus). Now Clamence tells his listener that the sky above Holland is full of doves, too high up to be seen. They would like to come down, "but here are only the sea and the canals, roofs full of shop signs, and not even a head on which to light." Here Camus again draws upon Christian symbolism, and although his book doesn't answer in Christian terms the problems are nevertheless essentially Christian. And few books of this century have so effectively—however ambiguously—probed the conscience of modern man and his guilt. Unlike the true existentialistes, Camus seemed to believe, as the very title of *The Fall* shows, more in something resembling original sin than existential man appearing on this earth as pure being. Original sin is perhaps too oversimplified a concept to consider here as being a major part of Camus's beliefs; actually, Camus seems to have been more of an essentialiste than an existentialiste.

Or perhaps Camus meant to use the concept of the fall in another sense, as in Baudelaire's poem "Mon Cœur mis à nu" ("My Heart Laid Bare"):

What is the fall?
If it is unity become duality, it is God who has fallen.
In other terms, was not creation the fall of God?

In January, 1960, Albert Camus, living in the town of Lourmain, in the Vaucluse, planned to go to Paris and had bought his railway ticket. But his friend Michel Gallimard, nephew of his publisher, Gaston Gallimard, appeared at Lourmain with a car containing his wife and eighteen-year-old daughter. He invited Camus to go north to Paris with them, and Camus put the railway ticket in his pocket. It was the fourth of January.

Those who know the roads of France know that French law permits automobiles to drive at speeds which other countries regard as nothing less than criminal. One wonders how absurd life is, or how much existence itself means, when people race along so madly. At Villeneuve-la-Guyard (Yonne), fifty-four miles south of Paris, Michel Gallimard's car flew off the road and smashed into a tree. It was a straight stretch of highway, and the automobile hit the tree with such force that the heavy engine was hurled forty-five feet. Gallimard was taken to a hospital fatally injured; his wife and daughter were less seriously hurt. But Albert Camus had been instantly killed.

In the preface to the reissue of *The Wrong Side and the Right Side*, Camus had said that he knew what was wrong with his early book, but that it was part of the process of self-discovery and that he would sometime find the way to say what he wanted and needed to say: "Yes, nothing prevents one from dreaming, even in the hour of exile, and so at least I am sure, with certain knowledge, that the work of a man is nothing else than this long journeying to recover through the detours of art the two or three simple and great images by which, at the first, his heart was opened. Perhaps that is why, after twenty years of effort and publication, I continue to live with the idea that my work has not even begun." Hélas!

GOOD NOVELS CONTINUALLY come out of France. In the postwar years, the most exciting, and often the best of these have been either existential fiction or that of the nouveau-roman (new-novel) school. Yet the quality of traditional or even of merely average French novels earns them some mention here, however briefly they are treated. A number of authors will therefore be discussed now, in a generally alphabetical way. Some of these writers are put in this section because they are unclassifiable; others are just popular.

One of them, by an unusual twist, has written in English: *The Crossing* (1964), by Alain Albert, born in 1943. Albert who published a volume of verse in French in 1960, was a friend of the American Negro novelist, Richard Wright, who spent the last years of his life in Paris. Albert, who became a jazz musician at fourteen, learned to speak the rough-and-ready English of members of American jazz bands and of American students, writers, beatniks, and soldiers. Albert, who is brownskinned, looking "something like a Yemenite Jew," was somewhat an outcast in the Norman village where he grew up; his schoolmates threw stones at him and his brother, calling them Moricauds ("Darkies"). So Alain Albert, knowing what it felt like to be an alien, was able to write an extremely convincing novel about a Negro, Dan Peebles, who is first seen in a Mississippi mental hospital (he had beaten up a young white man) from which he soon escapes. The book, with its violence, panic, and flight, has certain elements in common with Wright's *Native Son*, but it isn't extensively imitative. Its imaginative projection of the Deep South is a tour de force, but a remarkable one.

Putting Louis Aragon in a section that includes a number of traditional novelists may seem odd, since as a poet he belongs in the avant garde, as he does with some of his early novels. Yet *La Semaine sainte* (1958; *Holy Week*), a vast historical novel, belongs to a different category from *Le Paysan de Paris* (1926; *The Peasant of Paris*). Aragon insists that *Holy Week* is not actually a historical novel, that it only seems to be directed toward the past, for it is really a quest for the future. Yet it is a story of the Napoleonic era, specifically the week of March 20, 1815, the time when Napoleon had escaped from Elba and returned to shake France once again and all Europe. The story doesn't touch on Napoleon himself, but rather on the flight of Louis XVIII from Paris with his entourage. It is a crowded and colorful story, but even in its technique it turns back toward the past, for it is written in a mixture of the manners of Balzac, Stendhal, and Zola. And the descriptions of the confusion of that famous week are probably based on Aragon's memories of the rout of the French by the Germans in 1940. He has at any rate written a highly energetic, huge novel of history, with fine portraits of statesmen and soldiers and ordinary French men and women. The painter Théodore Géricault is among the central characters, as full of vital color as one of his own canvases.

Christine Arnothy, one of the talented younger writers, wrote a poignant story of adolescence in *J'ai quinze ans et je ne veux pas mourir* (1958; *I am Fifteen and I don't Want to Die*) and an icily analytic novel about a middle-aged woman in *Pique-nique en Sologne* (1960; *Picnic in Sologne*, translated as *The Serpent's Bite*). The pampered Yvette, who wants to perserve her beauty, has been married for many years to Gérard, who looks forward to having their son Philippe take over his factory. A former lover of Yvette's turns up, causing Gérard to doubt whether Philippe is his son. A quite different type of writer, the sharp satirist Marcel Aymé, brought out his first novel, *Brûlebois* (1926), when he was twenty-four. He first attracted widespread attention with a vigorous comedy about peasant life, *La Table aux crevés* (1929; *The Table for the Weary*), his fourth novel, which won the Prix Théophraste-Renaudot as the best novel of the year. Aymé became a prolific writer, and his novel *La Jument verte* (1933; *The Green Mare*) was frequently spoken of as Rabelaisian. He turned out some of his best work after the Second World War. In *Le Chemin des écoliers* (1946; *The Road of the Students*), the fates of three German soldiers of the Paris occupation are traced, through death and amputation and so on; the one who remained in Paris was caught alone by a street mob at the time of the liberation and torn to pieces. *Uranos* (1948; translated as *The Barkeep of Blémont*) is a fierce yet funny satire of the effect of the German occupation upon a small French town. Aymé has had considerable success in the theater since the war, and he is one of the finest of modern short-stories writers, as in the title piece of the volume, *Le Passe-muraille* (1943; *The Walker-Through-Walls*), in which a timid little bureaucrat discovers by accident that he can step through walls. He suddenly becomes a bank robber and jewel thief, leaving notes signed "the Werewolf" for the police, who finally capture him. But he slips through the prison walls, only to meet with disaster at the home of his mistress. In *Derrière Chez Martin* (1938; *Behind the House of Martin*), Aymé wrote a number of stories about a recurrent character named Martin, who is not necessarily always the same Martin; one of these stories, set in a boys' school, shows Martin accused of writing obscene graffiti on the lavatory walls and using the graffiti to make fun of the superintendent and his wife, but when the superintendent tries to identify Martin as the culprit, there is a little comedy of confusion. The tale "Knate" was published in 1936 in a volume by Théophraste-Renaudot prizewinners; it is, in one long paragraph, the hilarious monologue of the tailor Knate. "Josse" is a more serious story of a warrant officer retired from the army who goes to stay with his sister in a small town and sadly misses the barracks life. This tale is from the collection *En Arrière* (1950; *Backwards*), whose title story is one of Aymé's finest. It is an amusing fable about the sons of some Paris billionaires who join a young literary man (named, of course, Martin) in founding a magazine which celebrates capitalism and attacks the working class; but the boys change their tune when their rich fathers are outraged and cut down their allowances. It is a typical, lively, Aymé comedy.

In 1965 a first novel won the Goncourt Prize: Jacques Borel's *l'Adoration*, a somewhat Proust-like story of a sensitive boy who grows up in Paris before and during the Second World War. The adoration of the title is the fierce affection between Pierre and his mother, who goes mad when her son marries.

Yves Berger's *Le Sud* (1962; *The South*, translated as *The Garden*), a winner of the Prix Fémina, is like Alain Albert's *The Crossing* in that it is an evocation of America by a young Frenchman who has not yet seen the country. But it is a different kind of evocation, because it doesn't concern today's South, but yesterday's, Virginia of the 1840's as imagined by a man in the southern France of today. He makes over his house into the replica of a plantation mansion, with magnolias and wisteria. He has named his daughter Virginie and his horse Indiana; it is the son, whose name is not given, who tells the story. He has become entangled in his father's dream, and upon growing up starts to write a book about the Virginia of the 1840's. But his somewhat older sister refuses to sink into the fantasy. She takes her brother to live with her to attend the university in Montpellier, where she seduces him and brings him alive into the modern world. But gradually their intense love—whose physical aspects are described with Gallic carefulness—fades, and the young man returns to his father's "plantation." A dark and haunting book, it seems to make no definite point about attempts to catch time past. Atmospherically, it is reminiscent of Julien Green.

Another writer who is expert at atmosphere, though of a realistic rather than a fantastic kind, Jean-Louis Cotte, was born in 1923, son of an officer in the colonial army. He married a girl from Algeria and for a few years settled in that country, about which he wrote some color-charged stories. Cotte, who was for a time a Mediterranean fisherman, set his story *l'Appât* (1958; *The Trap*) on one of the Balearic Islands, a place of saltpans and screaming gulls. One of the principal characters is a half-crazed maimed man whom the islanders call King. His crippled mother carries a gun in her wheelchair, from which she sporadically fires away at the gulls. There is also a flashingly beautiful girl, loved by the Polish refugee who comes to the island to tell the "King" that his brother has been killed on the Spanish mainland. This brother supposedly left a treasure on the island, and two gangsters who had been associated with him come there in search of it. From one end to the other, *The Trap* is a story of violence and melodrama, and although the narrative moves rapidly across the events, it is handicapped by the unrelieved brutality of the story, which is too full of the unbelievable and of grotesquely superficial characters to keep the reader's attention very profitably engaged.

Representative of an uprooted generation, the Spanish-born Michel del Castillo writes in French, the language of the country in which he now lives. Born in Spain in 1933, his early childhood was spent in the midst of the Civil War which, he says, has scarred him for life ("It was on bloody scenes that my eyes first opened"). He was taken to France in 1939, among all the refugees from Franco's Spain. He was interned in a concentration camp in France, later in another in Germany, then was placed in a Jesuit school in Spain, from which he ran away to return to France in 1949. All these adventures are recorded in his first novel, *Tanguy* (1953), which was extremely successful internationally, known in English-speaking countries as *A Child of Our Time* (several times produced on

American television). *La Guitare* (1957; *The Guitar*) is a short narrative about a symbolic outcast, a dwarf, who fruitlessly seeks a little love so that he will not be in the category of monsters. The novel *Le Colleur d'affiches* (1958; *The Billsticker*, also translated as *The Disinherited*), based on the author's childhood recollections, attempts to tell a full-scale story of the Spanish Civil War. It shows the republic, set up with a democratic constitution, threatened by Communists within and by Fascists without. In the middle of this conflict, Michel del Castillo places three young men, two of them from the lower classes and one the son of a marquis. They all become Marxist warriors. But disillusion sets in: one of the young men, soon to die in battle, says that even if the republic wins, injustice will still exist. The marquis's son, whom both sides look upon as a renegade, is executed, and there is the suggestion that the third of them, tortured by Franco's henchmen, goes mad. The book contains excellent battle and hospital scenes, but its ideology is confused, as the loyalist leaders often were themselves. *Le Manège espagnol* (1960; *The Spanish Riding School*, translated as *Through the Hoop*) is a satiric picture of Spain after many years of Franco, with a Tartuffe-like clergy playing politics in a miserable country; unfortunately, Del Castillo, who was capable of compassion in *A Child of Our Time*, has too heavy a touch for satire, and he editorializes too much. The picture of greed and villainy is relieved by the presence of a truly Christian figure, Carlos Sanchez, who is murdered by the soldiery when trying to save an idiot from being wantonly killed. Another sympathetic figure, Father Risueño, serves to emphasize the futility of trying to be a good priest in a corrupt society.

Jean Cau, born under the shadow of the Pyrenees in 1925, won the Goncourt Prize in 1961 with *La Pitié de Dieu* (*The Mercy of God*). Cau, who was for several years secretary to Jean-Paul Sartre, is a star reporter on the Paris paper, *l'Express*. His novel, a kind of existentialist allegory, is a profound exploration of the nature of guilt.

It deals with four men forced to spend their days together in a prison cell: a boxer, a onetime choir boy, a crane operator, and a doctor. The reason that they are cooped up together is that they are murderers. In the daily horror of their confined lives, what they were guilty of, and what they were merely guilty of thinking, become confused. One of their amusements is to burn roaches, a game they call The Torture of Joan of Arc. Holding a lighted match to a captive roach, they exhort it to deny its sainthood and confess itself to be an instrument of evil. The doctor in the course of the story tells the others that they don't exist, that he is dreaming them; and they tell him that they are going to worship him as God. Cau's examination of the processes and results of guilt is often reminiscent of the imaginative writings of Camus and Sartre, though murkier, philosophically more muddled.

The Belgian-born Alexis Curvers (Liège, 1906) deserves mention for a pleasant little comedy about postwar Rome, *Tempo di Roma* (1957). Curvers has written other novels, among them *Bourg-le-rond* (1937, in collaboration with Jean Hubaux) and *Entre Deux Anges* (1955; *Between Two Angels*), but his masterwork is *Tempo di Roma*, which neatly catches the tempo of Rome, as seen and felt by Jimmy, an exile who has adopted it. He rapidly moves through a series of amusing episodes at all social levels. The story gives a fine view of Rome, with its teeming streets, its soft fountains, its rich gardens. The portraits of human beings are skillfully done, including Jimmy's girl Giovanna, as essentially innocent as her mother, Pia, is crafty. It is an engaging fable.

Maurice Druon, born in 1918, is best known for his cyclic novels. A veteran of the battle of the Loire in 1940, Druon escaped to England to broadcast for the BBC during part of the war, then went on to Algeria in 1943. After the liberation he became a writer. He wrote several novels about France in the Second World War, including *La Dernière Brigade* (1946; *The Last Detachment*), a story of the officer cadets who in 1940 attended cavalry school at Namur, some of them irritated when they learn they will be attached to the mechanized corps; when they go out to attempt to stop the Germans at the Loire, most of them are killed. The story, with its contrast between academic war games and the reality of battle, is told in an effectively terse style. Druon's six-volume series, *Les Rois maudits* (*The Accursed Kings*), covers French history from the reign of Philip IV (1285–1314) through the career of Philip VI, who became the first Valois king in 1328, as described in the last book in Druon's series, *Le Lis et le lion* (1960; *The Lily and the Lion*). Druon also wrote a trilogy about France between the wars, *La Fin des Hommes* (1948–51; *The End of Man*, translated as *The Curtain Falls*), comprising three volumes, the first of which won the Goncourt Prize: *Les Grandes Familles* (1948; *The Great Families*), *La Chute des corps* (1950; *The Fall of Bodies*), and *Rendez-vous aux enfers* (1951; *Rendezvous in Hell*). The trilogy tells the story of two prominent families bound by marriage, the landowning La Monneries and the Jewish bankers, the Schoudlers.

The central figure in these books is Simon Lachaume, whose intellectual brilliance enables him to rise above his peasant origins to high peaks of journalism and politics. But there is nothing heroic about Simon who, though he remains within the law, advances himself by means of chicanery and opportunism. He is an appropriate figure to help bring about the downfall of the two great families. The panorama of the story includes accounts of a climactic session in the chamber of deputies, of backstage intrigues at the great Paris theaters, of the inner workings of the army, of the lives of a great poet and a famous playwright, of some stirring stag hunts, and of a variety of love scenes presented with Gallic candor. As the book ends, in the early part of the Second World War, Lachaume accepts the vice-premiership just as his estranged wife, Marie-Ange, is at a château with her brother, Baron Jean-Noël Schoulder: "It was not the kiss of a brother and sister; it was the kiss of man and woman." Druon's trilogy is full of dramatic surprises which enliven its many and varied episodes, but in depth the story never quite matches the breadth of the books.

Luc Estang, born in 1911, won the Grand Prize of

Literature of the Académie française in 1962 as a reward for various achievements in poetry and the novel. His work is sometimes reminiscent of that of Georges Bernanos. His books of fiction include *Temps d'amour* (1947; *Time of Love*) and the trilogy, *Charge d'âmes* (1950–54; *Burden of Souls*), including the three volumes *Les Stigmates* (1950; *The Stigmata*), *Cherchant qui dévorer* (1951; *Seeking Those Who Devour*), and *Les Fontaines du grand abîme* (1954; *The Fountains of the Great Abyss*). These are religious novels of which orthodox Catholics disapproved. Estang is often didactic, and his people and plots rather mechanical. In *Le Bonheur et le salut* (1961; *Happiness and Safety*, translated as *The Better Song*), a middle-aged clerk, Octave Coltenceau, deserts his wife and two children to languish on the Riviera with a beautiful young widow, Marie-Laure; but at last his conscience begins to stifle him. The book ends with Marie-Laure cutting her throat. In the sequel, *Que ces mots répondent* (1964; *That These Words Might Answer*), Octave returns to Paris and is restored to his job and his family. Marie-Laure had left a note saying she killed herself to give Octave peace of conscience, adding that she realized he would also suffer. But he doesn't: his wife becomes sexually satisfying, his faith is bolstered by a priest, and even his recalcitrant young son is won over. But the "new" Octave, happy in his happy family, is hardly convincing, and the end of the story is, considering the moral issues involved, too blissfully smug.

Another of the younger novelists, Claude Faux, who once served as secretary to Jean-Paul Sartre, wrote a tuberculosis-sanatorium novel in *Les Jeunes Chiens* (1959; *The Young Dogs*). In 1924, Thomas Mann set an impossible goal for such a novel, with *The Magic Mountain*, at once a detailed picture of a limited community and a projection of the entire modern world. Yet the sanatorium setting still contains dramatic possibilities, as the Englishman writing under the name of A. E. Ellis showed in *The Rack* in 1958, and as Faux showed in his novel the year following. The young dogs of its title are the youthful patients of a sanatorium near Paris—some of them young enough to be continuing their studies—shortly after the Second World War. A few of them had been members of the underground; they chafe under confinement and often break out to seek wine and women, usually with damage to their health. Despite one death by hemorrhage and the piercing of a few needles, this book has less of the physical gruesomeness of disease than the Mann or Ellis volumes; and altogether the young dogs are an engaging group. Where the other books stressed the hectic eroticism of the patients, Faux's novel emphasizes their sexual impotence. The book, however, has no center of interest; neither any individual nor the group itself compels the reader into identification. But the story has some good individual episodes.

Louis-René des Forêts, born in 1918, has been a spasmodic writer. His first novel, *Les Mendiants* (1943; *The Beggars*), richly lyrical and on the grand scale, was followed by *Le Bavard* (1946; *The Chatterer*), a book of far more modest dimensions, and then, after a long silence, by the short three novels of *La Chambre des enfants* (1960; *The Children's Room*). Yet the color and theatrical force of his writing have kept his reputation high. Jean Forton, born in 1930, is a bookseller in his native Bordeaux. His first novel was *La Fuite* (1959; *The Flight*); his second, *Isabelle* (1959), won the Prix Fénéon. In *Le Grand Mal* (1959; *The Great Evil*, translated as *The Harm is Done*), Forton shows an uncanny understanding of the psychology of children. The setting is a harbor city shaken by the abduction of several young girls; a demoniac boy influences a weak friend to help him frame a gentle and innocent man who is then driven to his death. *The Harm is Done* is a grimly effective picture of the ferocity of which children are capable.

Russian-born Romain Gary (Tiflis, 1914), whose actual name is Kacewgary (also spelled Kassevagari), writes out of an adventurous career as a kind of minor André Malraux. Gary was brought up in Nice by the extravagantly emotional mother he describes in his autobiography, *La Promesse de l'aube* (1960; *Promise of Dawn*), which was dramatized for the New York stage (1962) by Samuel Taylor. Gary served with the air force before the fall of France and, after it, in North Africa with the Lorraine squadron of the Free French. He received the Croix de Guerre and other decorations. His first novel, *Éducation européenne* (1945; *European Education*, translated as *Forest of Anger*, revised in 1961 as *Nothing Important Ever Dies*), told the story of the Polish partisans during the war. It won the Prix des Critiques. Gary, who went into the French diplomatic corps, married the writer Lesley Blanch; his second wife is the American-born French film star, Jean Seaburg. Gary's second book, *Tulipe* (1946), is an overblown allegory. *Le Grand Vestiaire* (1948; *The Great Cloakroom*, translated as *The Company of Men*), is an examination of disturbed postwar adolescents, a story containing both comedy and sadness; it is somewhat in the tradition of *Oliver Twist*. *Les Couleurs de jour* (1952; *Colors of the Day*) is set in Nice at carnival time, and tells of the love affair between an American actress of French ancestry and a one-armed French veteran of the Spanish and Second World wars, doomed to meet his death soon afterward in a mine field in Indochina. The explosive colors of the Riviera carnival, the unhappy passion of a weak-spirited actor, and the murder of a Sicilian-American gangster are woven into the story which suffers from lack of focus, which remains cloudily between satire and pity. Gary won the Goncourt Prize with *Les Racines du ciel* (1956; *The Roots of Heaven*), the story of a man in Africa trying to save the elephants from obliteration. *Lady L* (1958) is a romantic, imitation-Gothic trifle. *Le Manageur d'étoiles* (1961; *The Manager of Stars*, translated as *The Talent Scout*) was another story of film people. This was followed by *Gloire à nous illustres pionniers* (1962; *Glory to Our Illustrious Pioneers*). In 1964, a collection of Gary's stories was published in America as *Hissing Tales*.

Pierre Gascar, born in Paris in 1916 of a family of peasant origins, spent five years as a Nazi prisoner in the

Second World War. His first novel, *Les Meubles* (*The Furniture*), came out in 1949, followed by *Le Visage clos* (1951; *The Shut Face*). His first success came in 1953 when his two collections of shorter work, *Les Bêtes* (*The Beasts*) and *Le Temps des morts* (*The Time of the Dead*), won the Goncourt Prize. These were published together in English as *Beasts and Men* in 1954. The principal story in *The Beasts* concerns the horses rounded up in the first days of mobilization; in *The Time of the Dead*, Gascar tells of his experiences in prison camp as gravedigger for his fellow captives who had died, and tells of this with cool objectivity. In his novel *La Graine* (1955; *The Seed*), Gascar takes as his subject the misery of a ten-year-old boy who loves Paris but is forced to live with relatives in a factory town in the country. In his lonely desperation, the boy poaches and gets into other trouble, until at last his father is sent for, and the meeting between the two, while not outwardly eventful, shows the boy his future; he realizes that he will have to discover reality for himself, "like a dog."

In *l'Herbe des rues* (1957; *Grass in the Streets*), Gascar again points up the conflict between Paris and the provinces, this time with politics and questions of war intruding. *La Barre de corail* (1958; *The Coral Bar*), written after Gascar visited Somaliland, was a highly erotic story that yet found time to denounce racism and colonialism. Gascar's style is sometimes swollen with rhetoric, but is more often genuinely poetical. *Le Fugitif* (1961; *The Fugitive*) is the story of a man who makes two flights. The first is from a German prison camp. After the war he marries the farm girl who has sheltered him, but when he can no longer stand the lingering nazism of his father-in-law, he makes his second flight. Paul pretends that he has been killed and wanders across Germany, becoming increasingly involved in the black-market and moral underground. In *Les Moutons de feu* (1963; *Sheep of Fire*), Gascar wrote a pleasant little comedy about a pro-Algerian group in Paris which hides its explosives in the stuffed lambs in a taxidermist's shop.

A forceful woman writer of the postwar era, Geneviève

Gennari came from a family that was Italian on her father's side; her mother was French. Born in 1920, she published her first book in 1947, her doctoral thesis on Madame de Staël. In 1949 Geneviève Gennari turned to fiction with *Les Cousines Muller* (*The Muller Cousins*), the story of three girls. In this volume that author showed that she had a shrewd eye for bourgeois manners as she told the story of the three girls from adolescence to maternity. She wrote several other novels of middle-class experience, breaking off to produce an example of historical fiction in *l'Étoile Napoléon* (1954; *The Napoleon Star*). Geneviève Gennari resumed her career of writing novels of modern France, one of the most notable of which is *Journal d'un bourgeoise* (1959; *Diary of a Bourgeois Woman*, translated as *The Other Woman I Am*). This is the story of a lonely young widow in her quest for self-discovery. In *Les Nostalgiques* (1963, translated as *Nostalgia*), Mlle. Gennari focuses on a well-to-do family of central France, observed by a Russian-born governess. There are two central woman characters in this book: the governess, Nathalie (Nastasha) Elikov, and one of the members of the de Trabert family, Diane. The story begins in 1938, when Nathalie comes to the château to tutor Diane's niece and nephew. A good deal of the narration is flashback, from the vantage point of the 1960's. Diane, married and divorced, has become an actress and marries one of her former teachers, the brilliant Jean-Pierre Lepic. Nathalie, now married to a banker, has become a writer who has gone through what she calls a "para-existential" period (Mlle. Gennari knows the extentialists at first hand and has written an important essay on Simone de Beauvoir). But Nathalie cannot rid herself of nostalgia for the days at the château and decides she can do so only by writing a novel about the de Traberts. Meanwhile Diane is trying to find her own identity in her marriage to Lepic. Geneviève Gennari writes of all this with great skill, compressing a family chronicle into a novel of ordinary size.

Marcel Haedrich's bestselling *La Rose et les soldats*

(1961; *The Rose and the Soldiers*, translated as *The Soldier and the Rose*) was a story written by an Alsatian and set in Alsace and Paris. Marc Waerlé, a young officer in the French army, goes to Paris after the collapse of France and there meets again Mathilde, the magnetic Alsacienne, who has forgotten him while she was busy becoming a star in the entertainment films made by the occupying army. The events of 1940, with the mixture of loyalties, are skillfully blent into the main story, which concerns the attempt of Marc and Mathilde to begin where they left off—but in the meantime, Mathilde has been intimately associated with the aging German director, Herbert von Kramenski. The novel is, for all the interest packed into its background material, a rather conventional one, and von Kramenski, with his limp, his closely clipped hair, and his monocle, is a bit too much of a stage German. One author writing in French who created a brouhaha was the Rumanian-born Vintilla Horia, author of *Dieu est né en exil* (1960; *God Was Born in Exile*), an imaginary journal of the Roman poet Ovid in exile in what is part of modern Rumania. When the book won the most distinguished of literary prizes, the brouhaha began: the Communist newspaper *l'Humanité* revealed that Horia, who had recently moved to France after several years in Spain, had before and during the Second World War written pro-Fascist and anti-Semitic articles for Rumanian newspapers. *L'Humanité* cited the articles, which Horia admitted writing. He then refused to accept the Goncourt Prize. Jean Hougron (born 1923) is a vigorous writer who deals in Malraux style with the East, particularly in his six-volume cycle, *La Nuit indochinoise* (1951–58; *The Indochina Night*), which is full of the brutality, heat, and suspense of jungle-fighting in the 1950's. In *Je reviendrai à Kandara* (1955; *I Will Return to Kandara*), Hougron evokes the atmosphere of colonial France and the life of a minor professor. Hougron writes in a clear style and in a tense manner. Another younger novelist, Jean-René Huguenin, who was born in 1936, wrote a highly effective narrative full of the atmosphere of the Breton shoreline, *La Côte sauvage* (1960; *The Savage Coast*, translated as *The Other Side of Summer*), a story of the fierce drives of incestuous instincts.

Le Veilleur de nuit (*The Night Watchman*) won the Renaudot Prize in 1962. It is a modern gothic novel: meshed in an internal dream, the narrative weaves back and forth in time, through and across horror. The night watchman, pushing his bicycle along the street of a town in Normandie and carrying on his mysterious excavations in an ancient house, is an intense and compelling figure. Siméon Leverrier, who lures a salesgirl into captivity, finds in his own destruction a release from the agonies of living. The book, in its dark ambiguity, has at times a Julien Green-like manner as well as one suggesting the nouveau-roman school; as a story, it has a horrifying effectiveness. The author, Simonne Jacquemard, is a noted ornithologist.

The uncle of Marcel Druon, Joseph Kessel, was born in the Argentine in 1898 and went to France as a young man. While he was studying at the Sorbonne, the First World War broke out, in which he became an aviator. Afterward he visited Russia and wrote *Le Steppe rouge* (1923; *The Red Steppe*), short stories about the reign of terror after the Russian revolution. *L'Équipage* (1924; *The Equipment*) was a story of wartime operations. Some critics think this is Kessel's finest novel, but his own preference is for *Belle de jour*, which came over into English untranslated because it means a special flower, convolvulus minor; it is in any event the name assumed by one of the characters, the beautiful Séverine. She is sexually schizoid, spending half of her time with her husband and half as one of the star turns in a brothel. Kessel's most ambitious attempt has been his tetralogy, *La Tour du malheur* (1950; *The Tower of Misfortune*), the story of the Dalleau family. The first volume of the series, *La Fontaine Médicis*, is the most effective, with its pictures of Paris and the western front in the early years of the First World War. Kessel's best-known novel is *Le Lion* (1958), an international success, a story in Africa against the background of Mount Kilimanjaro. The game warden of the area is a famous white hunter, John Bullitt, whose elfin daughter, Patricia, has a magic way with animals and forms a remarkable friendship with the lion, King. But when King and a native are in a death grapple, Bullitt reluctantly has to shoot the lion. Patricia, who has loved the game reserve as a paradise is bitter and disillusioned, and goes away to school and "civilization." The story is at times effective, with its pictures of the animals, but it is also often shoddy and superficial. Kessel became a member of l'Académie française in 1962.

Belgian-born José-André Lacour (born in 1919), began his career with a two-volume novel about the fall of France, *Châtiment des victimes* (*Punishment of the Victims*), a story of the war, defeat, and occupation. He has written several plays and several other novels, the most striking among the latter being *La Mort en ce jardin* (1954; *Death in that Garden*). This is the grim story of a group of people meeting their doom in an Amazonian rain forest. A former Nazi, a priest, an uprooted Jew, a soldier, and a diamond expert accompanied by his small deaf-mute daughter—the reader follows them all through the process of slow, horrible death. For it is horrible; few writers today have written so grisly a story. In the jungle, for example, the starving people are forced to eat snakes, which they can only vomit up. They at last find the crashed plane bearing gold which they have been seeking, but by this time it is too late; the last survivor turns to cannibalism. Nevertheless, in the course of the story, some of the characters have risen to a nobility of a kind little known amid the comforts of civilization.

Two women who have written quite different kinds of novels, Monique Lange and Françoise des Ligneris, reveal a deft touch in such books as *Les Platanes* (1960; *The Plane Trees*), by the former, and *Psyché 59* (1959), by the latter. Monique Lange's *The Plane Trees* begins in Paris, the sun glaring on the asphalt, and Claudia looking for the journalist, Diego, whom she loves. The actress who has been his mistress has left him, and he drives south in pursuit of her, letting Claudia accompany him part of the way. When they reach the languid South and its profusion of plane trees, Claudia tries to entice Diego to spend a night with her, but he refuses, and she takes the train back to Paris. Stepping out of the station, for the first time without luggage, she thinks: "I look like a whore who couldn't find any customers in Avignon." The prose of the story is taut and spare, yet it wonderfully conveys atmosphere and emotion.

Françoise des Ligneris' *Psyché* 59 is as deeply Gallic in its concentration upon the problems of love, but the author's touch on the page is somewhat less light though not less skillful. This is the story of a beautiful woman blinded by an accident. Mahaut, as the protagonist calls herself after the heroine of a novel of the medieval period, is bound in a slavelike relationship to her magnetic husband, Eric, who after the coming of her blindness becomes entangled with other women, one of them Mahaut's own sister, who has a habit of wearing flashing red skirts. The contrasting atmospheres of the world of blindness and brightness are neatly dramatized, and so are the female perceptions that become so important in this novel.

One of the publishing sensations of 1965 was *La Bâtarde* (translated into English with the French title retained), an autobiography by Violette Leduc. The book was called a récit—a story, narrative, or report—hence it passed as fiction; and it is certainly the product of an energetic imagination. It tells the gruelling story of a girl and young woman whose father did not acknowledge her; she was brought up by an angry and unaffectionate mother. It is a story full of exotic loves, often lesbian, plainly described. The heroine marries but, rather than face motherhood, causes herself to have a miscarriage; divorce soon follows, and she thereafter associates with men of a more neutral type. *La Bâtarde*, which is full of strong passion, is a startling revelation, a kind of female counterpart to some of Jean Genet's novels. Violette Leduc, who has also written several earlier books, is a writer of power. Some of her most effective passages in *La Bâtarde* concern her wartime experiences, when she became comparatively affluent in the black market. In her writing career, she has often been associated with the existentialistes, and Simone de Beauvoir has encouraged her.

A young woman writer of great talent who didn't live to witness the success of her only novel, Eveline Mahyère wrote *Je jure de m'éblouir* (1958; *I Vow That I Will Amaze Myself,* translated as *I Will Not Serve*). Undoubtedly autobiographical, it tells of Sylvie Ceyvenole's attachment to one of her teachers, Julienne Blessner, who gives up a promising career as an architect to become a novitiate in a convent. Julienne is in turn attracted to Sylvie, who comes to represent the temptations of secular life, so she breaks off the relationship. Once again a very young French writer has demonstrated an ability to render atmosphere, situations, and the inner workings of character in an intense story. It is the intensity that is particularly notable in this book, amid the setting of boulevards, Parisian attics, and cafés jammed with young intellectuals —an intensity apparently too great for its author to bear, for in her twenties she followed the example of her character Sylvie and killed herself.

A woman writer of still a different kind, although her first book had points in common with Eveline Mahyère's *I Will Not Serve,* Françoise Mallet-Joris was born in Belgium in 1930. She went to the United States for part of her education, which was continued at the Sorbonne. At nineteen she wrote a surprisingly mature novel, *Le Rempart des béguines* (1951; *The Bulwark of Bigots,* translated as *The Illusionist*), the story of a Belgian girl who has a lesbian affair with her father's mistress. Written in an almost classic style, in a frame of clear poetry, the book evoked comparisons to the Marquis de Sade, Choderlos de Laclos, and Colette. *La Chambre rouge* (1953; *The Red Room*) tells of the love adventures of a girl named Hélène in a story of tragic intensity. *Cordélia* (1954), a collection of short novels, presents in its title story a heroine, Cordélia, who tries to maintain a life of both bohemianism and purity; the hero in "Nathan Oppenheim" encounters death early in life and sees a resemblance between the corpse of his father and some fish in the refrigerator; "Le Souterrain" ("The Underground") shows how the force of childhood, buried in everyone, remains a living power; "Mort d'un village" ("Death of a Town") portrays the agony of *things*. In *Les Mensonges* (1956; *The Lies*, translated as *The House of Lies*), Françoise Mallet-Joris wrote abundant and lyrical descriptions of marriage preparations, in the story of the struggle between a father and his illegitimate daughter, who remains true to her mother and lets her father die without leaving her his fortune. The author continues this tone of richness and fullness in *l'Empire céleste* (1958; translated as *Café Celeste*), which won the Prix Fémina. In the story, a group of souls are condemned to live together forever like those in Jean-Paul Sartre's *No Exit*. *Les Personnages* (1960; *The Great People*, translated as *The Favourite*) is an unusual historical novel in that it is spare, not cluttered with the costumes or period furniture over which readers usually stumble. This book devotes most of its space (and it runs under three hundred pages) to clean action and sharp conversation. All this helps to heighten the effect of the fairly conventional story of Louise de La Fayette, mistress of Louis XIII and ultimately the victim of the intrigues of Cardinal Richelieu. The author's gifts of irony and psychological insight give further effectiveness to this story of the girl who, caught between the opposing forces of the Cardinal and of Louis's queen, Anne of Austria, is persuaded into a nunnery. There, in a passage of subtly wrought complexity, she discovers in herself a new identity. Françoise Mallet-Joris with this book brings an air of freshness in to the mouldy chambers of the historical novel.

Andrée Martinerie's *Les Autres Jours* (1960; *The Other Days*, translated as *Second Spring*) is the story of a thirty-three-year-old woman, married for ten years and the

mother of two children, who feels in bovaryste fashion
that her life is becoming routine. She engages in a love
affair with a fifty-year-old archeologist who is killed in an
automobile accident: one of the striking scenes in the
story finds the heroine, Geneviève, forced to attend a
theatrical performance, full of blood and violence, soon
after she learns of her lover's death. But Geneviève has
already realized that her destiny is with her husband, with
whom she now enters upon a "second spring" of marriage.
Andrée Martinerie, who has translated many English and
American novels into French, is capable of writing a deft,
sensitive, and absorbing story. Loys Masson, one of the
French authors who writes of exotic parts of the world,
was born in 1915 on the island of Mauritius in the Indian
Ocean. Masson began as a poet, and the prose of his
novels retains a high sense of the poetic. One of his
novels, *Les Tortues* (1956; *The Tortugas*), is full of the
magic of islands in warm seas. *Les Noces de la vanille*
(1962; *The Marriages of the Vanilla*, translated as *The
Overseer*) begins on the island of New Caledonia, where
the narrator is a member of a band of outnumbered
revolutionaries. Because their leader, Manolo, looks like
someone (the overseer of the title) in the narrator's
childhood, his memories go back to Réunion Island when
he was eleven years old and, in a half-innocent, half-
worldlywise way, in love with a primitive little girl. Then,
as overseer to the boy's plantation, the satanic Esparon
arrived and brought evil into this tropical paradise. The
French critics who have compared Masson to Conrad and
Melville—because of his lyric prose and his ability to
dramatize evil as a part of nature—have not been reaching
toward too-far-fetched conclusions.

Albert Memmi's *La Statue de sel* (1953; *The Pillar of
Salt*), followed by *Agar* (1955), is representative of the
French literature of North Africa, whose most dis-
tinguished representative was Albert Camus; there are a
number of others who might be mentioned, including
Abdallah Chaamba, Driss Chraïbi, Mohammed Dib,
Assia Djebar, Mouloud Feraon, Mouloud Mammeri, and

Malek Ouary, all of whom have made interesting contributions to Franco-Arabic letters; one of these writers of Arab stock, Kateb Yacine, will be considered in a later section, among the practitioners of the nouveau roman (new novel). Just now, to return to Albert Memmi, who was born in Tunis in 1920; *The Pillar of Salt*, whose action takes place in that city, is the story of a poor Jewish boy who at school falls in love with French culture and abandons his hereditary background. When the Germans occupy Tunisia he realizes he can have no chance for an academic career; he is everywhere an alien: to the Nazis, to the Vichy French, to the Arabs, and to the Jews whose religion he had renounced. He leaves for the Argentine, watching the African coastline fade away into darkness as the stars begin to come out; and he is a pillar of salt.

Robert Merle, born in Algeria in 1908 and partly educated in the United States, won the Goncourt Prize with his novel *Week-end à Zuydcoote* (1949; *Weekend at Dunkirk*), which in 1965 was made into a Twentieth-Century-Fox film starring Jean-Paul Belmondo. The central figure in the story is a philosophy teacher, Julien Maillat, one of the French soldiers caught on the beach at Dunkirk. The English refuse to evacuate them, though because Julien can speak English some officers befriend him and put him aboard a boat which, however, is sunk in the low water, so that Julien as to return to shore and his comrades. Two soldiers try to rape a fifteen-year-old girl, the only member of her family left in her house, so Julien kills them; but then he forces her himself. The end is one of horror: as Julien and Jeanne are together in the old house, it is smashed by the Germans' bombardment, and just before Julien dies he finds that the top of Jeanne's head is crushed, after which he goes into a delirious dream of death. Merle, who was himself at Dunkirk, was captured by the Nazis and imprisoned for three years, wrote also in a naturalistic vein about his prison experiences in his novel *La Mort est mon métier* (1953; *Death is My Trade*). He also has written a historical novel, *Île* (1961; *Island*), and several of his plays have been produced, including *Flamineo* (1950) and *l'Assemblée des femmes* (1957; *The Assembly of Women*). Robert Merle is a professor at the University of Toulouse.

Hubert Montheilet, a detective-story writer, whose book *Les Mantes religeuses* (*The Praying Mantises*) won the Grand Prix de la Littérature Policière, brought crime-fiction talents to a new and higher level with *Le Retour des cindres* (1961; *Return from the Ashes*), the story of a Jewish woman doctor who comes back to Paris in 1945 after two years' confinement in a Nazi concentration camp; because she has contracted venereal disease in the camp's brothel—volunteering for service was her only means of insuring that she stayed alive—she goes to a sanatorium for a cure before calling on her husband. Since she has not reported immediately after the camps were opened, he assumes that she is dead. He enters into a liaison with her illegitimate daughter, who is nearer his own age than her mother. When they see her in Paris after her return, they notice that the haggard woman bears a resemblance to the missing doctor, so they invited her to join a conspiracy which will enable them to secure the estate of the supposedly dead woman. The story, told for the most part in the diary of the returned wife, is one of high horror, ending in a murder, an imprisonment, and a suicide. The novel is full of ironies; for one, the husband is a chess Grand Master, yet he sometimes makes the wrong move, as when he strangles in a railway compartment a man he assumes is a Gestapo agent, but who is actually a brothel owner. This husband, who has not even told his wife he is Jewish, has betrayed her to the Nazis after she has gone into hiding. The striking recognition scene, in which he discovers that the apparent impostor is really his wife, occurs during a chess match, when he finds that she can play expertly. As a story of disguised or mistaken identity—the imagination has to stretch a bit to imagine both husband and daughter not recognizing the wife and mother—*Return from the Ashes* is in the tradition of two highly popular pieces concerned with the First World War: Leonhard Frank's bestselling German novel, *Karl und Anna* (1927), and Luigi Pirandello's Italian play, *Come tu mi vuoi* (1930; *As You Desire Me*). In 1965, *Return from the Ashes* was made into a United Artists' film starring Maximilian Schell, Samantha Eggar, and Ingrid Tulin.

Michel Mohrt, born in 1914, the year one world war began, took part in the second, and wrote a rather breezy narrative of his experiences on the Italian front in 1940, in the novel *Le Répit* (1940; *The Respite*). *Mon Royaume pour un cheval* (1949; *My Kingdom for a Horse*) is a novel about the collaboration, while *Les Nomades* (1951; *The Nomads*) is a story of European exiles in the United States, a subject Mohrt knew at first hand from his teaching experiences at Yale and other American universities and colleges. Mohrt won the Grand Prix du roman of the Académie française for *La Prison maritime* (1961; *Mariner's Prison*), an imaginative story in the traditional manner told in retrospect by a man who, as a schoolboy in the 1920's, had become a seaman aboard the ship "King Arthur" at a time when he and his fellow-nationalists of Brittainy hoped to break away from France and help form a Celtic empire with the Irish and Welsh. The actions of the dashing Captain Kersangar and his crew lead to imprisonment, with light sentences, after a trial that, as presented, makes gentle fun of Gallic legal procedures. Indeed, in this book comedy rivals the adventurous aspects which are reminiscent of Joseph Conrad and Robert Louis Stevenson. One notably comic figure in the story is the sea-going priest known as Father Jib. But the most striking character of all is the glowingly beautiful Irishwoman, Lady Cecilia, who becomes the narrator's lover. In one highly comic episode they are locked up in a first-class compartment during a trip aboard a train. The episode is summed up in the narrator's satirically Victorian comment, "The reader may easily imagine how this sentimental journey ended." In *Mariner's Prison*, Michel Mohrt consistently worked a dead vein of tradition, for the people and situations are clichés, encountered many times before, but the tale is told without self-consciousness, and readers who don't insist on newer methods, with cubes peeping around corners at them, have found this novel pleasant reading for both its comic and adventure sequences.

Another Breton-coast adventure story also won the Grand Prix du roman de l'Académie française: Henri Queffélec's *Un Royaume sous la mer* (1957; *The Kingdom Under the Sea*). This is the story of Captain Jean Modénou and his relationship with his crew and with his wife, Madeleine. In a season of despair, the captain achieves a triumph when he finds a new fishing ground, the kingdom under the sea of the book's title. Then, after a man has doubly betrayed him—by revealing the secret of the sea and making love to Madeleine—Modénau summarily condemns him to death in the deep. But, as one particularly dramatic scene shows, there are some human emotions stronger than jealousy or revenge or a verdict of a kangaroo court; and a desperate voyage through choking fog is partly a voyage of self-discovery for Jean Modénau. Queffélec, who was born in Brest in 1910, has written several other novels, including *Combat contre l'invisible* (1958; *Fight Against the Invisible*, translated as *The Men of Damezan*), the story of French scientists racing to catch up with those of other nations in developing atomic power. The protagonist is Michel Renoir, a résistance veteran now trying desperately to get the reactors working in the provincial plant at Damezan. His dedication to his work, which he feels his wife doesn't understand, has turned him into a man of steel. His story, which includes a love affair with a Damezan girl, is a compelling one, with fine insights into the problems involved in such dedication as these "new men" represent.

Albert Palle's *l'Expérience* (1959; *Experience*), which won the Prix Renaudot, is the story of a man evoking is past. At sixty-two, the newspaper reporter Pierre Balagneux arrives with a colleague at a seaport town to write up the suicide of a young man. Pierre is continually reminded of the harbor city in which he grew up (Palle is a native of Le Havre), effectively evoked in his memories of youth.

The voice and laughter of a barmaid in the town where the suicide occurred remind Pierre of a Greek prostitute he had been in love with just as he was coming out of adolescence; but the barmaid Geneviève seems to have no connection with the Greek girl Kara, who during one of her nightly cabaret acts showed signs of madness and had to be put into an asylum. The reporters never discover the truth of the suicide they have come to investigate, though Pierre finds some of his own lost youth in the town and decides to stay there. The story is often confusing, full of false leads and of episodes not dramatically explained, but atmospherically it is often compelling.

Better known as a shocker than as a serious writer, though parts of his fiction have been highly praised, Roger Peyrefitte (born 1907) has spent much of his life in the diplomatic corps. His novel, *Les Amitiés particulières* (1944; *Special Friendships*) is an unusually candid account of adolescent homosexuality flourishing in a Catholic college. The book won the Prix Théophraste Renaudot. Peyrefitte's ironic short novel, *La Mort d'une mère* (1950; *The Death of a Mother*), referred ironically though not always effectively to an experience in the author's own family. *Les Ambassades* (1951; *Embassies*, translated as *Diplomatic Diversions*) and *La Fin des ambassades* (1953; *The Last of Embassies*) were thinly veiled fictional accounts of the author's experiences as a diplomat. *Les Clefs de saint Pierre* (1955; *The Keys of St. Peter*) mingles the documentary and the imaginative in a story about Rome and the Vatican. Peyrefitte, who is a smooth stylist, usually lacks the inventiveness that has to go into a first-rate novel; he is generally more satisfactory in his Mediterranean and Aegean travel books. He has sometimes been compared to Anatole France, possibly not exactly a compliment. Peyrefitte, perhaps not altogether to his displeasure, became the center of a whooping scandal in 1964 when scenes of *Special Friendships*, not concealing what the special friendships were, appeared on television. The occasion was attacked as degenerate by seventy-nine-year-old François Mauriac, who besides being one of the principal Catholic writers of this age is also an ardent admirer of Charles de Gaulle, whose biography he wrote. Peyrefitte counterattacked, not only mocking at Mauriac as a Gaulliste, but also saying that the man had no business criticizing a portrayal of homosexuals, since he was one himself—an accusation made in the weekly *Arts* and then reprinted in most of the newspapers in the country, which reveled in Mauriac's silence. Peyrefitte said that Jacques Chabonnes, who followed Mauriac as president of the Société des Gens des Lettres, had urged that Mauriac be exposed as "the most colossal intellectual fraud of this century." The French have always taken literature seriously, as everyone knows; sometimes they can turn it into an interesting dogfight, though in this case M. Mauriac apparently decided the accusation was too absurd to require an answer.

For *La Nature du prince* (1963; *The Prince's Person*), Peyrefitte dug into sixteenth-century Italian archives to find his story of the erotic tribulations of Don Vincenzo Gonzaga, Prince of Mantua, whose first marriage was cancelled because it wasn't consummated, though whether this was attributable to the incapacity of the new husband or his princess-bride was difficult to discover. After an interfamily wrangle, involving a number of prominent churchmen, the Farnese girl was removed to a nunnery. But before Don Vincenzo could be married again, this time to one of the Medici, he had to prove himself as a lover, before witnesses. A virgin was procured to serve for the occasion, with results that Peyrefitte turns easily into sexual comedy, with all being well that ended well. The story enabled the author to make a few more mischievous attacks upon the Church. But he was more than mischievous, and in no way genuinely comic, in his next book, *Les Juifs* (*The Jews*), in 1965. This novel got to the roots of the anti-Semitism that has been at least latent in France since the Dreyfus case (and of course earlier). More thesis than story, the book attempts to unmask the "unknown Jews," such as General de Gaulle, who had some ancestors named Kolb—and there are three

Kolbs in *Who's Who in World Jewry*. For so large a book, the story itself is thin: it concerns a Goldschild family, easily recognizable as the Rothschilds, who are also mentioned by name in the book. Young Baron Saül de Goldschild plans to marry a gentile girl, Osmonde de N., who has several interviews with her future mother-in-law which give Peyrefitte a chance to exercise his talent for the scabrous. Madame Goldschild questions Osmonde with uncomfortable intimacy about her natural functions and eventually makes a pass at her. The girl eludes this advance and goes on to marry Saül. Meanwhile, the author floods the book with discussions of "le milieu d'Israël" and obsessively continues to point out public figures who have "Jewish ancestry." In July, 1965 the Rothschilds brought Peyrefitte into court, but a judge ordered that only one page be changed in order to obviate a suggestion of illegitimacy. Peyrefitte grinned, and sales soared: the book disappeared so fast from the shops that it was difficult to obtain copies of it. Peyrefitte, obviously with tongue in cheek, said that in trying to make Jews into the majority he was helping to bring "the Jewish problem" to an end. But as the Jewish writer Bernard Frank said in the journal *Candide*, the book was devoutly anti-Semitic, "a monstrous cocktail in a concentration camp."

One of the wartime novelists, Raymond Queneau is another of those authors difficult to place. He writes poetry as well as fiction, and is the author of a good deal of dancing light verse. Born in Le Havre in 1903, he attended the lycée there before going to Paris, where he took his degree in philosophy at the Sorbonne in 1925. He was a member of the surréaliste group, from which he broke away in 1929. Meanwhile, he had served with the Zouaves in North Africa; after his return, he became a bank clerk, teacher, journalist, translator, and editor (for the publishing firm of Gallimard, of which he later became a director). His first novel, *Le Chiendent* (1933; *Trouble*) was hailed at once as a comic masterpiece. *Trouble* tells the story of a bank clerk named Étionne

Marcel and his struggle with ideas of being and nonbeing. One of the features of the book is an elaborate war between France (once again called Gaul) and the Etruscans. *Trouble* is a varied book, written with linguistic virtuosity, definitely showing the influence of James Joyce's *Ulysses*. Queneau's wartime success was *Pierrot mon ami* (1943; *My Friend Pierrot*). In *Odile* (1951), Queneau savagely satirizes André Breton and other former associates among the surréalistes. *Un Rude Hiver* (1939; *A Hard Winter*) is the story of a First World War love affair between an English girl, serving as a WAAC, and a French officer. *Le Dimanche de la vie* (1952; *The Sunday of Life*) is the story of a young husband with a middle-aged wife, each of whom keeps a shop—what the people of the neighborhood confide in the husband, he passes on to his wife, who attains success as a fortune teller. When Julia has a stroke, Valentin dresses like a woman, wears a veil, and successfully replaces her. Most of Queneau's later work shows the lingering influence of surréalisme, blent with his own brand of wild comedy, as in *Zazie dans le métro* (1959; *Zazie in the Subway*), the hilariously trouble-making adventures of a small girl in Paris who succeeds in upsetting entire arrondissements, as indeed the book itself did, since Zazie is adept at picking up and repeating the salacious expressions she hears in the corrupt circles into which she is taken (her uncle is a female impersonator and exists in the half-world of the sexual and racketeering underground). What Zazie, the country girl, most wants is to ride on the subway, paralyzed by a strike; when at least the strike is over, Zazie is too exhausted to appreciate her first subway trip. One of Queneau's cleverest books is *Exercices de style* (1947; *Exercises in Style*), in which the same episode—a minor incident on a bus—is narrated in ninety-nine different ways: laconic, florid, Italianized, Anglicized, hyperbolic, and so on, a satiric pastiche of methods of composition. It is a book which is supposed to have taken Queneau ten years to write.

One of the odd novels to come out of France in recent

years is *l'Histoire d'O* (1954; *The Story of O*), which recounts the adventures of a Parisian girl taken by her lover to a kind of brothel of a very expensive sort, where she is kept chained. Tortures are inflicted, by whipping and by burning. The author, who writes under the name of Pauline Réage, is in the tradition of the Marquis de Sade and of Leopold von Sacher-Masoch—though the eminent French critic Jean Paulhan of the Académie française and long an editor of the *Nouvelle Revue française*, states in an essay on the book that it is foolish to look for masochism in it. He finds its essential quality to be a "pitiless decency." The girl known as O submits without protest to everything, and in a one-sentence alternative ending the author suggests that O prefers to die than to be left by Sir Stephen, one of the men in the house where she is chained. The book, published by the Olympia Press, is in any event a curious exploration of various channels of eroticism, and its success has been enormous, particularly in the English translation sold to tourists. It is at the very least another manifestation of the variety to be found in the contemporary French novel. The story is presented forcefully enough to be gripping, and such horrors as it contains are emblematic of a large part of modern life.

In 1962 Henri-François Rey received the Prix Interallié for *Les Pianos Méchaniques* (*The Mechanical Pianos*), which in 1965 was filmed in its setting, the Costa Brava of Spain, with Merlina Mercouri and James Mason. The central characters of the story are the enchanting, sophisticated, middle-aging Jenny, proprietor of a popular bar, and Régnier, also middle-aging, a French novelist who chases young women. The latter are rather easy to pick up along the Costa Brava, according to this story, and one of the most attractive of them is one whom Régnier calls Orange. Neither he nor anyone else in a village that is a magnet for people speaking many languages can determine what tongue Orange speaks; but Régnier keeps her on until his small son, usually tolerant of his father's amours, sends her packing. Anyhow, the rainy season has started, and Orange is glad enough to go, for she can be happy only in sunlight. And then the unusual happens, for Régnier stays in the town beyond the season. He and Jenny form an alliance that promises each of them a warm autumnal glow, for the season and for life. Heretofore they have been like the people who frequent Jenny's bar, who are symbolized by the mechanical pianos of the title; their tune is loneliness. The story has several subplots, notably one concerning the love affair of two adolescent children, which has disastrous results. The author has an annoying habit of switching on the stream of consciousness of various characters, using parentheses to do so—this is often jarring, though sometimes the book makes for smooth reading, and the atmosphere of the decadent resort is effectively conveyed.

A woman author who has made a strong impression with her controversial first novel, Christiane Rochefort just missed receiving the Prix Fémina for *Le Repos du guerrier* (1958; *Warrior's Rest*). It at least caused a terrific battle between the forward-looking and backward-thinking women jurors, who finally awarded the prize to another excellent book, the previously mentioned *Café Céleste* of Françoise Mallet-Joris. The Académie Goncourt also squabbled over Christiane Rochefort's *Warrior's Rest*, which didn't go without laurels, for it won a newly created award, the Prix de la nouvelle vague (Prize of the New Wave). *Warrior's Rest* concerns Geneviève Le Theil, a young woman of Paris, and Jean-Renaud Sarti, who is in his own phrase an idealist in a vacuum. Renaud had been in his late teens as the Second World War ended in Europe, and he faced the future with hope until the bombing of Hiroshima. Ten years later, in a small-city hotel, he tries to kill himself by drinking poison. Accidentally blundering into his room, Geneviève finds him unconscious and, sending for help, saves his life. She later calls on him at the hospital and despite his violent bitterness, becomes fascinated by him, at least physically. Then she, who has been a virgin, becomes Renaud's lover, and they travel to Switzerland and Italy on an extended and destructive spree that is not without its bitter humor. Renaud is the warrior of the title, the fighter against what he thinks are false values; there are too many of them, and he becomes the opponent of life itself. But finally Geneviève's obsessive love for Renaud (she is going to have a child by him) makes him want to rejoin the human race, and he insists that she marry him; man is the miscarriage of a monkey, Renaud says, but adds that he himself has been the miscarriage of a man; and he insists on trying to rehabilitate himself by going to the clinic he calls the Great Washing Machine. There is an odd similarity between the ending of *Warrior's Rest*—at least in the unmarried Geneviève's pregnancy—and the termination of Christiane Rochefort's *Les Enfants du ciel* (1961; *Children of Heaven*), but the couple involved in the latter is quite different. Philippe is a television-installation man, and young Josyane is a product of the new government-assistance epoch (the first phrase in the book is, "I was born of the family subsidies"). There is much talk of work-interruption phases of social security as Josyane's mother carefully plans to have children in relation to the single-salary allotment. Josyane, growing up in a housing project and filled not only with slogans about it but about all aspects of life (the Citroën has a road-holding capacity), asserts her fundamental humanity through adolescent sex adventures. But when she becomes pregnant by Philippe, whom she genuinely loves, she reacts like the mother she has contempt for, and tells Philippe that after they get married they can, because of the expected child, get a government loan. These books of Christiane Rochefort are not great novels but, like so much French fiction today, they are superior to most written elsewhere: her work is sharp and penetrating, with emphatic contemporary significance.

Often compared with Raymond Radiguet, and justly so, Jean-Baptiste Rossi was only nineteen when he finished *Les Mal-partis* (1950; translated as *The False Start* and as *The Awakening*), the story of an adolescent boy's love affair with a nun; the final scene at the railway station, where two priests tear the boy out of the arms of his mistress, is particularly effective and affecting. The poet Robert Sabatier, born in 1923, has written several novels of Montmartre, including *Alain ou le Nègre* (1953; *Alain, or The Negro*), *Le Marchand de sable* (1954; *The Dealer in Sand*), *Boulevard* (1955), *and Canard du sang* (1958; *The Bloody Duck*). Of these, *Boulevard* (winner of the Prix de Paris) may be taken as typical, the story of the French equivalent of the angry young man, a scrounging adolescent who lives near Place Pigalle, in a single room of a mouldy tenement where he exists, or tries to, from the potatoes he cooks in a bucket on his woodburning stove; Georges has many adventures in the district, but the great moments of his life occur when he goes up to the tenement roof and watches the cafés light up their signs above the glowing Boulevard de Clichy—an occupation Georges varies by spying on his fellow tenement-dwellers through the roof's skylights.

The most sensational and famous of all the younger French novelists is, of course, Françoise Sagan, born in 1935. She scored her first success, an international one, when she was nineteen, with *Bonjour tristesse* (1954), the story of a young girl, Cécile, who retains a curious naïveté despite having been brought up in a sophisticated manner by her father; but Cécile can react with the full ferocity of a jealous woman, and although the story is thin on plot, the people themselves are well plotted out, in a style at once terse and tense. In *Un Certain Sourire* (1956; *A Certain Smile*), young Dominique, who already has a lover of her own age, is confronted by a middle-aged seducer. In her two short novels which followed, *Dans un Mois, dans un an* (1957; *In a Month, in a Year*) and *Aimez-vous Brahms?* (1959), Françoise Sagan, again with precocity and a chaste style, showed how unhappiness and loneliness cast their haunting shadows across pleasure seekers. In 1960, she scored a remarkable success in the theater with *Château en Suède* (*Castle in Sweden*), the wittily presented story of the marital troubles of an eighteenth-century couple whose female member continually seduces male cousins who visit the castle. Françoise Sagan's novel *Les Merveilleux Nuages* (1961; *The Wonderful Clouds*), set in Key Largo, New York, and Paris, is the story of an American painter who is jealous of his young French wife, whom he sets detectives to watch. Josée finally tells Alan that she has been unfaithful to him, describing "what the apartment looked like, how [Marc] had undressed her, their positions, their caresses, what words he had uttered when he took her, a special demand of his afterward." Alan is sorry he has heard these details, but Josée says she couldn't keep going as she was, and now "the game" is over. But "for a long while they stayed as they were, close to one another, like two wrestlers, exhausted."

The troubles of youth are the subject of a novel by a somewhat older author, Michel de Saint Pierre (born 1916), in *Les Nouveaux Aristocrates* (1960; *The New Aristocrats*). Among his earlier novels, *Les Aristocrates* (1954; *The Aristocrats*), with its fine portrait of the proud old Marquis de Maubrun, won the Grand Prix du roman de l'Académie française. In *La Mer à boire* (1952; literally *The Sea to Drink*, but meaning *A Difficult Matter*), Saint Pierre wrote about war at sea. Earlier, in his first novel, *Ce Monde ancient* (1948; *This Ancient World*), Saint Pierre had written of two young men; one, at eighteen, loathed the Sorbonne and hoped to become a novelist, while the other was a proponent of social justice. The two young men stood together in condemning what they called the ancient world of injustice and shoddy values, harshly satirized in the novel. But a Jesuit father sounds a note of moderation in addressing the Sorbonne student: "The bourgeois world disgusts and irritates you. Very well! It disgusts you a bit too much, let me tell you! . . . You are all the more severe in regard to your milieu because you do not know others. Men are feeble and miserable, Giles."

A priest also speaks important words in *The New Aristocrats*. Father Philippe de Maubrun, teaching at the Pierre Favre College, tries to save the scholastic career of a brilliant but rebellious boy. He might have succeeded if the standards of the school were not too harsh; the boy writes an anticlerical, atheistic essay for the school paper and is, like the young Shelley, expelled. Father Maubrun pleads on behalf of the boy, but the rector of the college is adamant and, when Philippe quotes to him from Scripture the passage about saving the sheep that has gone estray out of the flock of a hundred, the rector answers with casuistry. Saint Pierre, in a foreword to his book, asks for tolerance of what he calls the new aristocrats, boys like the one expelled, who will be the élite of the future; they are not tricheurs (tricksters), he says, but sensitive and restless spirits who want the world to have more than mere happiness.

The Belgian-born French writer Georges Simenon is best known for his novels about Inspector Maigret, who has been for many years the favorite sleuth of highbrow readers. Simenon has written some seventy Maigret books, and more than three hundred and fifty works of fiction published under pseudonyms. But he has also turned out more than one hundred and eighty serious novels, many of which have won him high praise throughout Europe. André Gide went so far as to place him in the front rank of modern French authors, though Henri Peyre has said that the difference between Simenon and several other minor French writers "and their greater French contemporaries is a difference of intellect as well as imaginative power." Simenon is essentially a miniaturist, dealing with small situations, yet he often writes interesting stories with characters that hold the attention. Most of his novels are unrelievedly grim, even the ones penetrated by Maigret's dry humor. Among those classified as serious, *Dimanche* (1959; *Sunday*) is typical: it is the tense story of a chef in a small Riviera hotel owned by his wife whom he tries to poison and, in so doing, brings about a disaster he hadn't counted on. In *La Neige Était sale* (1948; *The Snow was Black*), a young man in an unnamed country in the grip of a Nazi-like army murders one of the occupation troops and is caught and executed. The autobiographical *Pedigree* (1948) deals with a child and his family living in comparative poverty in Liège: Roger Mamelin is shown growing up in the years before and during the First World War, with whose end the book ends, with Roger at fifteen (Simenon had intended to write sequels but was discouraged by the lawsuits this volume, considerably modified in later editions, brought on). *Striptease* (1958) bares the odious lives of cabaret girls in Cannes. *In Les Anneaux de Bicêtre* (1963; translated as *The Bells of Bicêtre*), Simenon won both popular response and critical approval with a story of a man struck down by a serious illness who has to take stock of his life. In 1965, Simenon again won both popular and critical acclaim with *Le Petit Saint* (*The Little Saint*), perhaps his finest serious book (but who can have read them *all*?). The title of the novel comes from the name given by his schoolmates to the central character, Louis, who is not actually a saint but has some of those characteristics, including meekness, which make the consecrated so difficult to have around in everyday life.

Most of the book concentrates on Louis's childhood and adolescence in the 1890's and in the early years of this century. It is an authentically grimy picture of life as it buzzes on in the midst of an ancient world-city, in the streets behind the places, boulevards, and gardens which the tourists know. The principal setting of the story is the narrow and grubby rue Mouffetard, a bit to the southeast of the domed Pantheon where some of France's heroes are enshrined. The rue Mouffetard existed in Villon's cramped little Paris, it bristled with Jacobins in the eighteenth century, and in our own time Hemingway has graphically described it. Simenon in his intimate view of the life there doesn't omit squalid details. In the little space in which Louis grows up—a tenement room with several children who don't know which of them might be legitimate or which of their mother's visiting lovers might be their fathers—the family chamber pot plays a hideously emphatic rôle, and pubescent perversions flourish among the children. Yet their mother is, in her feline way, a devoted mother, trudging every morning down to and across the Seine to the great markets of Les Halles, pushing a cart that she fills with vegetables to sell on the rue Mouffetard to keep the strange little family going. Most of the children leave, but are forever handicapped by their smudged beginnings. But Louis—who never really grows up, for he remains at five feet three-quarters of an inch—toughly survives in that Latin Quarter environment, and if he has one saintly quality in his meekness, he has another in that he loves all life. From internal compulsion, and without formal training, he becomes a painter, something on the order of the members of the Fauves (Wild Beasts) group that Simenon has always admired; he can convey in a few deft word-strokes the effect of Louis' savagely individualistic painting, which ostensibly brings him fame almost within the shadow of the Pantheon. The last part of his career, his progress into manhood (the overcoming of sexual shyness) and artistry, is rather hastily and at times vaguely sketched in. Too many of Simenon's books crumble toward the end or close with a jolting abruptness. But *The Little Saint*, like some of the others, deserves the reader's gratitude if only for the current of life that goes so wonderfully through most of the story. The character of Louis is touchingly attractive, and if he is at one level alienated from the community as a special man, he is at other levels not apart from it because he is an intensification of what is good in the community. His story is at once lively, realistic, genial, and magnetic.

A novel in the form of a dialogue which brilliantly examines the problems facing the world of today, Pierre-Henri Simon's *Portrait d'un officier* (1958; *Portrait of an Officer*, also translated as *An End to Glory*), is more than a dialogue, for it is full of character and action; but above all it searches out the reasons why nations are behaving as they are. France is the instrument of this examination, the France of the Second World War and of the subsequent colonial troubles in Indochina and Algeria. One of the questions this book raises is the treatment of the captured enemy—in these emphatic emergencies, with guerrillas peppering away at one in the jungle, does one torture and kill prisoners? Does the need for immediate information justify wrenching it out of captured men, however many lives it will save on the captors' side, and however justified their own case may be in comparison with that of the prisoners? But this is only one of the questions dealt with in this book, as part of the investigation of our larger morality and of all our activities in these schizoid years. The story is screened through the experiences of Jean de Larsan, a hereditary soldier; one of his ancestors was ennobled by Louis XV, during the Seven Years' War, and ever since then a Larsan has served his country, in royal, imperial, or republican armies. But this latest Lieutenant de Larsan has developed the Hamlet-like habit of thinking too precisely on the event. The result is a book of complication and profundity, a successor to Pierre-Henri Simon's earlier novels which explored the problems of Christian democracy, such books as *Les Raisins verts* (1950; *The Green Grapes*) and *Elsinfors* (1956).

Russian-born Henri Troyat won the Goncourt Prize with *l'Araigne* (1948; *The Spider*), the story of a vicious young man who preys upon his mother and sisters. Troyat, who was born in Moscow in 1911 and has become a member of l'Académie française, came to Paris in 1920; he has specialized in writing cyclic novels. The background of his Russian boyhood provided the material for the trilogy, *Tant que la Terre durera* (1947–50; *As Long as the Earth Shall Last*, translated as *My Father's House*). A single volume, *La Neige en deuil* (1952; *The Snow in Mourning*, translated as *The Mountain*), tells of two brothers—one fiercely avaricious, the other gently kind— who search for an airplane that has crashed in the Alps; unfortunately, a lovely woman from India who is among the passengers brings a far-fetched symbolism to an otherwise tense and absorbing story (Spencer Tracy played in the American film of it). Among cycles, Troyat's longest so far is *Les Semailles et les moissons* (1954–58; *The Seeds and the Harvests*, translated as *The Seed and the Fruit*). These five books begin with the

Limousin peasants, Pierre and Alamie Mazalaigue, who move to Paris and operate a café in Montmartre, then later become hotel keepers in Mégève; the early novels deal with their love, courtship, and marriage, and the later volumes center on their daughter, Élisabeth.

The third book in the series, *Élisabeth*, deals with the childhood adventures of the Mazalaigue's daughter, lonely in Paris because her parents can spend little time away from the busy café. In adolescence she is sent to a girls' school, where she is unhappy and rebellious. Finally she becomes ill and goes to recuperate at the home of relatives in the South, where she attends her uncle's school for boys. She has felt sex rise in her when a boy named Georges glanced at her admiringly, making her "feel as if she were wearing lipstick and silk stockings and high-heeled shoes," but she learns another side of the game when a boy she is attracted to, Martin, ignores her.

In the next volume, *Tendre et Violente Élisabeth* (1957; *Tender and Violent Elizabeth*), the heroine marries a young musician with whom she is not really in love. Instead, she violently, tenderly, and illicitly loves a man older than herself, who is physically attracted to her but cruelly unconcerned about her as a human being. The scene is set against the striking background of the ski resort at Mégève, which alternates with Paris and the grim circle of Élisabeth's relatives by marriage. Unfortunately, much of the story is written at low pressure, in a fairly conventional way, and the people tend to be types, though often interesting ones. Élisabeth's surprisingly firm self-assertion at a Swiss hospital at the end of the book gives it a conclusion with some dramatic strength.

The final volume, *La Rencontre* (1958; *The Encounter*) picks up the story of Élisabeth some time after her divorce from Patrice Monastier and takes her through the Second World War. She drops the older man who has become her lover and marries Boris Danoff, a Russian émigré who works in the French underground. In many ways this is the most vital book in the series, with its

dramatic accounts of occupied France. Too often, however, the writing is flat, although Élisabeth herself
emerges as a full-bodied creation.

Henri Troyat has continued writing cycles of novels
with a new one set in the age of Napoleon and swinging
back and forth between France and Russia, in the series
La Lumière des justes (*The Light of the Just*), in such
volumes as *Les Compagnons du cocquelicot* (1959; *The
Brotherhood of the Red Poppy*), *La Baronne* (1960; *The
Baroness*), and *Les Dames de Sibérie* (1962; *The Women
of Siberia*). Here Troyat uses a sweeping canvas, but as in
most of his books it is filled with large spots of dullness. In
1965 Troyat brought out *Les Eygletière*, which takes its
name from the modern French family the story deals
with; this is the first volume of a new series. Perhaps the
most popular novelist in recent France, Troyat has the
gift of inventiveness and can present a full gallery of
differing characters, but all too often the writing is
unfortunately no more than commonplace.

One of the most exciting authors to come up since the
war is Roger Vailland, who died in 1965. He was born in
Paris in 1907 of a Savoyard family. Vailland, who began as
a surréaliste, became a Marxist and belonged to the
underground during the German occupation. He wrote a
fine, piercingly humorous novel about that underground
in *Drôle de jeu* (1945; *Jesting Game*). He won the
Goncourt Prize with *Les Mauvais Coups* (1949; *The Bad
Blows*, new edition 1959, translated as *The Turn of the
Wheel*), a story showing the influence of the writer of the
past for whom Vailland has often expressed admiration,
Choderlos de Laclos; Vailland wrote a modernized screen
version of Laclos' *Les Liaisons dangereuses* (*Dangerous
Liaisons*), the last film of Gérard Philipe before his
unexpected death (he played opposite Jeanne Moreau).
Vailland's *Turn of the Wheel* shows how a collapsing
marriage is invaded by a beautiful young girl who brings
disaster, but without avail to herself, for although the
husband in the case says he loves her, he leaves her—a
rather un-Gallic touch that the author is able to make

convincing because he has made the character of the husband, Milan, complex and convincing. Likewise, Milan's wife Roberte is intensively portrayed, as is Hélène, the rather innocent assistant schoolmistress who causes all the trouble. As customary in a Vailland novel, the setting—this time a village in the Savoy where the local drink is a brandy called marc—is neatly sketched in. But the most important feature of this book is the savage conflict between Milan and his wife, ending in her driving off drunk into a pond. After his return to Paris, Milan is asked by one of his business associates how Roberte is, and he answers, "Roberte remained in the village."

In *Un Jeune Homme seul* (1952; *A Young Man Alone*), an engineer deserts the middle class because of a bad conscience and goes to the people to preach communism. After several other books, Vailland brought out *La Loi* (1957; *The Law*), regarded as his finest since *Jesting Game*. *The Law* again brought him the Goncourt Prize. The action of *The Law* takes place in Italy, in semi-feudal Porto Manacore, in which the local potentate, Don Cesare, has control over the virtue of the local girls, but there are other villains held up to scorn in this book, including the gangster Matteo Brigante and even the streetcorner juvenile delinquents. Vailland's objective is apparently to show the evils of the bourgeois world in contrast with the Communist.

His *Fête* (1960) is an altogether different kind of book: like André Gide's *The Counterfeiters*, it uses the novel-within-a-novel technique. The central figure of the story is Duc, a middle-aging novelist who proposes to the young wife of a friend that they have a "fête." This means going away together, which they do over the feeble protests of the young woman's husband and with the compliance of Duc's wife. After the man and the girl have spent some time at a provincial hotel and she returns to Paris, Duc begins to write a novel about the affair, and *Fête* itself ends with his putting onto paper what the reader will remember as the book's opening passage—baffling because the reader can't quite know where fact begins and fiction leaves off. But if the story itself is an old one, and rather conventionally Gallic, it is at least notable for the lifelike portrait of the young woman involved. Vailland knows her intricately, with a French-male shrewdness.

The illustrator Robert Bruller, who writes fiction under the name of Vercors, became well-known among the war writers, particularly as the author of *Le Silence de la mer* (1942; *The Silence of the Sea*). He has kept up his career as a novelist with *Les Armes de la nuit* (1946; *The Arms of the Night*) and its sequel *La Puissance du jour* (1951; *The Power of the Day*); *Les Animaux dénaturés* (1952; *The Cruel Animals*, translated as *You Shall Know Them*); and *Colères* (1956; *Rages*). Perhaps Vercors' most charming story is *Sylva* (1961), somewhat of a reversal of David Garnett's attractive novella, *Lady into Fox*. In *Sylva*, the protagonist, Richwick, while watching a fox hunt at the edge of his estate in England, is astonished to see a vixen who is fleeing from the hunters turn miraculously into a young woman. Richwick tries to domesticate Sylva, as he names her; she has a wild smell, resents baths, and eats out of her plate, but he persists, gradually falling in love with her and losing his "human" girl, who in her frustration returns to drug addiction. Sylva now and then runs away into the woods, driving Richwick frantic, but she keeps returning and at the last seems on the way to becoming a normal girl. In this Ovidian tale, Vercors shows unusual skill at depicting the temperament of the fox-become-girl, her coyness, her occasional flashes of savagery, and her essential and magnetic femininity. The story draws upon old sources of myth and legend and offers various allegorical meanings, but above all it is a charming story, full of neatly comic touches.

An extremely unusual author, Marguerite Yourcenar, is known chiefly for her *Mémoires d'Hadrian* (1951; *Hadrian's Memoirs*), which she helped to translate into an exemplary English version. It is unusual among historical novels—not in the way that Françoise Mallet-Joris' *The Favourite* is, by disposing of what in the theater are called properties, but rather by making them an important part of the story, though not obtrusively so. Indeed, the virtue of *Hadrian's Memoirs* is its internal quality, suggesting that the author has really penetrated deep into the mind and heart of the emperor. It is one of the few distinguished historical novels of the age, a marvelous imaginative projection of imagined memoirs. Marguerite Yourcenar's *Coup de Grâce*, which she also helped translate from the French, is somewhat less successful; written in 1939, it deals with people living on the great estates in the Baltic area just after the First World War, when the White Russians were fighting the Bolsheviks. It is a color-filled and rapidly moving story, but it lacks the depth of *Hadrian's Memoirs*.

This section might have included many other competent and skillful French novelists, among them Raymond Abellio (Jean Soulès), Hervé Bazin, Henri Bosco, Jean-Louis Curtis, Julien Gracq, Jean Malaquais, Robert Margerit, Roger Nimier, Louis Pauwels, Emmanuel Roblès, Else Triolet (Mme. Louis Aragon), and others, but this could go on almost forever because the French have so many good writers. Numerous other novelists will be discussed, however, among the new-novel authors.

5   ANTILITERATURE LITERATURE

1 *Chosisme: The Focus on* Things

New ideas and techniques invaded French literature in the 1950's with a group of writers dedicated to what has been called alittérature (nonliterature); they often produce the antiroman (antinovel) or indulge in chosisme (which might be literally translated as thingism). Another name frequently applied is l'école du regard (the school of the look). In their novels and manifestoes, the antinovelists emphasize their escape from the conventional novel's preoccupation with straight-line plot, psychological analysis, and moral involvements. The group of chosistes concentrate on material objects because, in the words of one of their practitioners and spokesmen, Alain Robbe-Grillet, "things *are there*." He says that literature has never really explored even their surfaces.

These doctrines, and the books giving flesh to them, appeared at a time when fiction all over the world was becoming abstract and bodiless. Authors of the immediate past such as James Joyce, D. H. Lawrence, and Marcel Proust had a notable concreteness in their work, but their kind of writing was no longer offered. There was occasional description, in novels and stories, of the conventionally realistic kind: the cataloguing of properties in, say, a room in which action was taking place. But objects merely listed don't have the solidity, the color, the livingness of objects as presented in the writings of the older authors mentioned above, or in the works of the chosistes. The traditional novelists, however, often gave their readers nothing except a sketchy indication of place, with dialogue. Now it is true that dialogue (reduced to a minimum in Robbe-Grillet's work) can be highly effective, as Nathalie Sarraute finds Ivy Compton-Burnett's to be; but for the most part the antinovelists of France have provided living backgrounds for dialogue. In traditional novels the effect that life makes on the consciousness was lost: there were no chairs that could really be sat in, there were no windows looking out on trees that were green, with sunlight rich on their shaking leaves. Novels were tombs of dead words.

The chosistes, if they have done nothing else, have restored a sense of concreteness to fiction. Their exclusion of other elements of the novel might be questioned, as well as the manipulation of their technique, which is perhaps not always successful; but at least the chosistes have made readers aware, once again, that they step daily through a world of solid objects (the cubes, cones, and cylinders of Cézanne), of glowing colors, of vital movement. But the chosistes have also done something more: they have, even in their failures, made their material seem exciting.

The nouveau-roman writers have been extensively criticized for not dealing in realist or naturalist fashion with the problems of postwar France, such as the crises that occurred in Indochina and Algeria, and the rise of Charles de Gaulle to omnipotence. These writers receive particularly harsh treatment from Simone de Beauvoir in *Force of Circumstance* (1963). Yet these new novelists reflect, in their own way, the chaos and terror of the epoch.

The antinovel school first manifested itself in the 1940's, notably with Nathalie Sarraute's second book, *Portrait d'un inconnu* (1947; *Portrait of a Man Unknown*). One of the ancestors of the school is Jean-Paul Sartre, largely because of his novel, *La Nausée* (*Nausea*); and it was fitting that he introduce the original edition of the *Portrait*; also fittingly, he used the term antinovel to describe what Mme. Sarraute and several other writers were doing with (or to) the novel.

2 Nathalie Sarraute and the Age of Suspicion

A member of a Jewish family, Mme. Sarraute was born in Russia in 1902 and has lived in France since early childhood. In her student days she attended several foreign universities, including Oxford, where she spent a year. The mother of three daughters all associated with the arts, Mme. Sarraute is the wife of a prominent Paris lawyer; she practiced law herself until 1939, the year she brought out her first novel, *Tropismes* (*Tropisms*). This series of prose sketches, often reminiscential, shows her already using some of the antinovel techniques, particularly in the general namelessness of the characters. But although the writings of Mme. Sarraute share this and several other characteristics with the chosistes, she is not actually a member of their group; her work does not manifest their intense concern with *things* as such.

The Sarraute book with the preface by Sarte, *Portrait of a Man Unknown*, caused little stir when it came out in 1947, but it brought fame to its author when the house of Gallimard took it over and reissued it in 1956. That was also the year in which Mme. Sarraute published her notable essay, *l'Ère du soupçon* (*The Age of Suspicion*), which attacked the traditional novel and even such modernists as Virginia Woolf, whom the author dismisses while praising a less-known English novelist, Ivy Compton-Burnett. Beginning her book with a statement by Stendhal—"The genius of suspicion has come to the world"—Mme. Sarraute puts Joyce and Proust into a past age and decries the use of "psychology" in the novel. She believes that the imaginative writer, whether attempting to entertain or to reform his contemporaries, must as honestly as possible "scrutinize, with all the sincerity he can summon up, as far as the acuteness of his vision permits, what seem to him to be reality."

Portrait of a Man Unknown suggests a lampoon of the traditional mystery story. The only named character, the narrator Dumontet, who is a kind of amateur detective, spies on a father and his aging daughter, vigilantly watches their commonplace behavior, and at last invades their lives. He has actually discovered nothing except their nagging and drabness. His ultimate action becomes this mystery novel's surprise ending: he suddenly marries the daughter.

The story is presented with complicated intensity, working its way through the barely perceptible or merely nascent impulses of the characters, the smaller feelings that come before the larger ones, the emotions that probe and withdraw, then probe again. All these Mme. Sarraute designates—in the biological word for the instinctive movements of organisms—as tropisms. French literary circles refer to them as sarrauteries, a term first used by Claude Mauriac.

Martereau (1953) is centered in the vision of a sick young man whose illness, like so many maladies of our time seems partly self-willed. This young man is a concentration of the characteristics of the oversensitive: those who are splintered by their own complications, people loving and hating at the same instant. In this case, tubercular fevers magnify the character's faults as well as his virtues. His complications, along with those of the total situation, make *Martereau* the best, the most fully developed, of Mme. Sarraute's novels.

The young man is the narrator of the story, telling of his uncle's friend Martereau, the only character in the book who has a name. Martereau is given some money in order to buy a country villa for the uncle, who is indulging in tax fraudulence. The nephew, who likes Martereau, or believes he does, begins to implant suspicions in others about the way Martereau is using the funds. The result is hectic embarrassment and violent confusions. The story takes the reader through tortuous and sinister adventures of the consciousness.

So does *Le Planétarium* (1959; *The Planetarium*). Once again the action is limited to a few small points: the attempt of a young couple to take over an elderly relative's flat; the efforts of the male member of the couple to avoid a gift of leather armchairs; the despair a woman feels at what workmen have done to a door. Mme. Sarraute, writing of all this in the present tense and using a variant of the stream-of-consciousness method, sufficiently heightens her effects to make all parts of the material seem emphatically and equally significant. The book differs somewhat from her others in that the people are given names, if somewhat grudgingly; and the story is related in the third person rather than in the first.

The Planetarium swept France, where it was a best seller for more than two years. If anything, its success showed that the public, as well as the sophisticated critics, had become responsive to the antinovel. Mme. Sarraute's contribution—in this book her absorption with interior decoration has almost a chosiste flavor—might be called the exploration of the sub-psychological. But this is just another word for her own term, tropismes. In *Les Fruits d'or* (1963; *The Golden Fruits*), Mme. Sarraute writes about a best-selling novel of that name, in a tenuous satire on literary circles which becomes almost a parody of her own method.

3 Robbe-Grillet and the Magnetism of the Object

Alain Robbe-Grillet began as an agronomist, serving the French government in equatorial Africa and in Martinique. He brought out his first novel, *Les Gommes* (*The Erasers*) in 1953, when he was thirty-one. He at once became one of the antinovelists, eventually the leading apostle of chosisme.

Like Mme. Sarraute and other alittérature writers, Robbe-Grillet professes to avoid using the customary properties of the novel, such as plot, psychological development, and message, respectively the favorite devices of the classicists, the realists, and the social or religious propagandists. Similarly, he shrinks away from the metaphors and symbols so dear to the romanticists and symbolists. Robbe-Grillet is particularly opposed, in poetry and prose that draw upon nature, to what Ruskin called the pathetic fallacy, which attributes human characteristics to inanimate matter, as "the cruel, crawling foam" or "Now sleeps the crimson petal, now the white." In order to escape such anthropomorphic reductions of experience, Robbe-Grillet projects events with an unemotional, geometrical precision and measures landscapes and objects with compasses and calipers. In this refusal to humanize objects, he presents them scientifically and descriptively—and they dominate his story.

The ancestry of Sartre in the history of the new novel has already been mentioned: an ancestry not of his existential ideas, but rather of the technique as used in *Nausea* (which has its own odd ancestry, Rilke's *Malte Laurids Brigge*). Robbe-Grillet, in an essay, "Nature, humanisme, tragédie" (in the *Nouvelle Revue française*, October, 1958), says that although Sartre claimed to have avoided the personification of objects in *Nausea*, he really failed to do so. The answer must be made, however, that Sartre attempted to do so, and that he was, in that novel at least, pointing the way toward chosisme. Robbe-Grillet in the same essay also says that Camus, in his own first novel, *The Stranger*, was likewise unable to refrain from giving objects a personal force; and it is true that, in the last part of that book, landscape and seascape and sun seem to behave personally toward Mersault, as when the sun "searches" his eyes. Nevertheless, Robbe-Grillet has admitted that the first part of *The Stranger* had an influence upon him; and he also lists, as an ancestor, an obsure and eccentric writer, Raymond Roussel, who died in the 1930's. Philosophically, Edmund Husserl (1859–1938), the phenomenologist, seems to stand behind such antinovelists as Robbe-Grillet. As John Cruikshank notes in *The Novelist as Philosopher* (1962), "Although academic philosophy often clung to abstraction and seemed indifferent to actual human experience, phenomenology was preaching a return to more concrete thinking with Husserl's slogan: 'We want to get back to things-in-themselves.'" And, as Laurent Le Sage observes in *The New French Novel* (1962), "The new novelists' rejection of the analytical method of presenting characters is postulated upon the same philosophic rejection of identity that motivated Edmund Husserl in the first years of this century to reject neo-Kantism. . . . For a Robbe-Grillet, who repeats Sartre's exultant cry that interiority is abolished and that things *are* before they are something, there seems nothing left but the human eye roving over the world."

Robbe-Grillet's *The Erasers* is a detective story. Inspector Wallas goes from Paris to a provincial town (anonymous) to protect an economist, Professor Dupont, who has been shot at by a gunman at a time when terrorists are assassinating prominent men all over the country. After arriving at the town, Wallas buys an india-rubber eraser, and while he is in the shop another man comes in and makes a similar purchase. This may be—just may be—the gangster. The significance of the erasers is never quite made clear; since the author preaches so ardently against symbolism, they can hardly be construed as symbols, except perhaps as parody, like so many elements of this book. On the other hand, Robbe-Grillet's method may not at this point (1953) have been sufficiently worked out so that he could altogether avoid symbols, any more than he could avoid metaphor, as when the proprietor of a bistro, reflected in its mirrors, suggests a fish in an aquarium. Even the eraser Wallas asks for is "une gomme très douce"—an eraser that is soft (or gentle).

But most of the story foreshadows the later Robbe-Grillet manner. The townscapes are done in firm geometry. Yet the detective story's fog of mystery sometimes softens them, as on the morning when Wallas gets lost in the mist that endows distances with "a new quality no longer related to geometry." Wallas, indeed, has been sent into a fog by his superiors, for at their request Professor Dupont, recovering in the hospital after being slightly wounded in the arm by the gunman, permits a government bureau to make it known that the victim of the attempted assassination has died. Wallas, ignorant of the fact that Dupont is still alive, goes quietly to the professor's house one evening to carry on his investigations. Dupont arrives to pick up some papers he needs, and Wallas, thinking he is the assassin, shoots and kills the man whose supposed murder he was probing. This is only one of the ironic reflections of the plot of *Oedipus the King*, which is subtly evoked throughout: the drunken old man Wallas meets in the bistro puts to him, in effect, the riddle of the Sphinx. The brand of eraser Wallas asks for in the shop he can describe only from a memory of one he has had before, on which all the letters printed by the manufacturer had been worn away except the middle ones—*di*—which has suggested to some readers that Wallas was looking for an "Oedipus" eraser.

The parody here is often comic, as it is in Nathalie Sarraute's *Portrait of a Man Unknown*, for it is also a lampoon on the detective story. But these authors were doing far more than indulging in burlesque; in each case they were finding their way toward a method.

By 1955, with *Le Voyeur* (*The Voyeur*), Robbe-Grillet, now a seasoned contriver of chosiste effects, had every *thing* under control.

The central figure of *The Voyeur* is a man who sells watches. In his thirties, he makes a three-hour voyage from a mainland port to the nearby island of his childhood; it is an unnamed island whose inhabitants have French names and wear sabots. While Mathias is there, a young girl is raped and murdered—or is she? Mathias, obsessed with young girls, with pieces of string, and with the flying gulls he keeps watching, might be the murderer —if there was a murder. The story is another puzzle, but one which closely involves the reader because what happens in it happens intensively through the slow, sure, repetitious projection of material things upon the consciousness.

Mathias' temperament gives one clue to the title: psychosexually, he is the voyeur, the scoptophiliac, the girl watcher, especially the watcher of little girls. Psychopathologically, the voyeurism is merely an extension of a normal male trait; a man's eye is erotically developed in a way that a woman's is not, so that most men are in some small way Peeping Toms; in the man who goes far enough in this direction to be extreme, voyeurism becomes an overt sexual manifestation, and there is little question that Mathias is of this type. But there is something more here: it is through Mathias' eyes that the reader is given the whole story of everything that happens—except, of course, the murder itself, if murder there was. Robbe-Grillet makes his reader the one who sees; in Laurent Le Sage's previously quoted words, "there seems nothing left but the human eye roving over the world."

It is time for an example of Robbe-Grillet's writing. Early in *The Voyeur*, when Mathias is aboard the boat, he has, among the graphic sensations of the moment, a childhood memory of himself sitting at home intending to do his school mathematics problems but, instead, drawing a picture of a gull he saw outside:

Something was missing from the drawing, although it was hard to tell precisely what. Mathias came to the conclusion that something was either not drawn correctly—or was missing entirely. Instead of the pencil, his right hand was holding a wad of string he had just picked up from the deck. He looked at the group of passengers before him, as if among them he hoped to find the owner of the material approaching him, smiling, to ask for its return. But no one paid attention to him or his discovery; they all kept their backs turned. A little to one side, the small girl seemed to be forgotten. She stood against one of the iron pillars that held up the deck above. Her hands were held together behind the small of her back, her legs braced and slightly apart, her head leaning against the pillar; even in so rigid a position as this the child retained something of her gracefulness. Her face glowed with the assured, yet conscious gentleness which the imagination attributes to obedient children. She had been in the same position ever since Mathias first became aware of her; she still looked in the same direction, to where the sea had been and where the vertical embankment of the pier now rose above them— quite nearby.

The transition from the boy drawing at home to the man on the deck of the boat holding the string is abrupt, an example of simultaneity and of Robbe-Grillet's "Einsteinian mixture of time and space," which the critic Roland Barthes has spoken of. The passage also provides a good example of Robbe-Grillet's ability to present and dramatize *things*. Several of the dominant, recurring objects of the story appear in that paragraph; the gull has been established as the subject of the boy's picture; the boy, like the man he becomes, is a hoarder of string; and he sees little girls through an erotic vision. The point that the little girl Mathias sees on the boat has her legs spread is made not only in the passage quoted, but elsewhere in the book as well.

The watches Mathias sells, or tries to sell, emphasize the time element in the story; and the time itself is continually noted by the author, as it is in the roman-policier type of book he was in part parodying. To add to the mystification, the time of the little girl's death is the one time not strictly accounted for in the unraveling of Mathias' consciousness; and whether his visions of the supposed or actual murder of the thirteen-year-old shepherdess are memory or imagination, the author never makes clear. Mathias behaves like a guilty man, but after three days leaves the island without jeopardy, boarding the boat at "four-fifteen exactly." A long passage describes the departure circumstantially, in elaborate physical detail, with the usual Robbe-Grillet geometry. The last object scrutinized is a buoy, precisely depicted: its shape is conical, it has a square turret and four uprights held together by crosspieces; there is a cylindrical cage with vertical bars, there is a main axis, and there are three triangles described exactly as equilateral, with horizontal bases. But in spite of all this display of mathematical properties, the substructure of the buoy, below the water, becomes a mélange of dancing shapes, intensifying the mystery as Mathias ends the book by reflecting that in another three hours he will be back on the mainland.

This technique of imposing lines, planes, cylinders, and ovals upon the consciousness of the reader as they are imposed upon the minds of the people in the story is carried on in Robbe-Grillet's next novel, *La Jalousie* (1957), which is perhaps mistranslated, in its English version, as *Jealousy*. Robbe-Grillet's third novel takes place on a banana plantation, evidently reflecting the author's experiences in equatorial Africa or Martinique: the vegetation that abounds in the area becomes an important actor in the story.

It is not told in the third person, like *The Voyeur*, yet *Jealousy* is not precisely in the first person either. There is only a recording consciousness, or rather an absorbing eye; and there are snatches of dialogue. Through these devices alone, a powerful story is told, or at least suggested.

The registering consciousness, represented by that detail-devouring eye, has only the identity of a husband who is a plantation owner; he is given no name. His wife, like a character in an antiquated novel, is known only by her initial, A.... The other figure in the story is designated as Franck; he is a neighboring plantation owner, and he may nor may not be making love to the wife of the first man. Since the story is that anomalous thing, a first-person narrative which never uses the *I*, it will perhaps be best to refer to the husband, or his projected consciousness, as The Eye, which at least has the merit of suggesting the impact of this character—who is, in the strictest sense, not really a character.

These explanations may make *Jealousy* seem more difficult than it really is. The reader will soon make his own way into the technical maze of the book, and if he persists he will probably find the story—if story it is—fascinating. It is circular and full of repetitions; it is a tale told by a camera that continually goes back over the same rows of objects and suggested situations.

The story, which occurs entirely in the present tense (*The Voyeur*, usually in past tense, occasionally switches into the present), starts with the description of a corner of a plantation verandah. A column supporting the roof—specifically the southwest corner of that roof—bisects that part of the verandah. In the beginning was—geometry.

Accenting the importance of the physical, the author provides a frontispiece map of the plantation house and some of its surroundings, including the ever-present banana trees on the road to the highway. The drawing includes a detailed diagram of the house, as in some detective stories; this one even shows the spot on the wall where a centipede is smashed, an event that has some ominous and recurrent function in the story.

What there is of story itself is simple enough. The Eye seems murderously jealous of Franck who, early in the book, has come for dinner "again," leaving his pregnant wife at home. The narrative, if such it may be called, indicates an intimacy, at least a sympathy, between A... and Franck. When he says he has to go away on a business trip to the port town, A... announces that she will accompany him, to do some shopping. They do not return when expected, but a day later, explaining that the car has broken down. They have spent a night at a hotel, but whether they spent it in the same bed is not possible to decipher from the story; The Eye's suppressed rage is as great as if they had. The centipede that was smashed on the plantation wall becomes smashed again in the hotel where the couple stay; or so The Eye "sees" it.

The scrambling of chronology in *Jealousy* imposes special burdens on the reader. There is, for example, "the body" mentioned, toward the end of the story, as halfway over the balustrade next to that roof-supporting column described at the beginning of the book. Is the body there as the result of a murder carried out by The Eye, or is it something imagined in the recesses behind the eye itself?

In spite of such puzzlement, many readers have felt that they have, in reading *Jealousy*, been taken through an intense experience, one indeed as intense as may be found in many far more comprehensible books, and more so than is afforded by the usual traditional novel.

Robbe-Grillet's *Dans le Labyrinthe* (1959; *In the Labyrinth*) is once again a mystery, this time with something of the flavor of a Franz Kafka story. Here the labyrinth is a city whose puzzling streets, projected forcibly as a living entity, dominate the story. The central human figure is a soldier who has come into the city after the army of which he is a member has lost an important battle; throughout, he knows that the enemy may enter the city at any moment. But he carries on with his mysterious quest: to deliver a package given to him by a dying friend. The messenger doesn't know what is in this cardboard box— some trivial letters—but he has promised the other soldier to carry it to a relative in the city. Wounded and exhausted, the messenger goes through the snow-choked streets, continually meeting a mysterious little boy and continually haunted by a street lamp whose zone of light is carefully demarcated.

As in the case of Kafka, critics have tried to read into this quest—the soldier's weary attempts to deliver the package—an allegory of modern man, lost in civilization. But Robbe-Grillet was apparently writing only another chosiste story, in this one letting the vast puzzle of the city be the dominant thing. The ultimate death of the soldier—if he actually dies—seems almost incidental in the white maze of baffling houses the city presents.

La Maison de rendez-vous (1965; *The House of Assignation*) is set in Hong Kong, chiefly in the large blue "house" of the title. One of the leading characters is an American, and it is interesting to see him against, or rather enmeshed in, the intensified scenery and the plot elements of a spy mystery whose resolution is, as usual in a Robbe-Grillet novel, a matter of guesswork. Also as always, objects—often fragmented as well as solid—are important, and the mystery of what happens blends into the mystery of personality.

In Robbe-Grillet's novels, his essays, and in such ventures as the screenplay he wrote (*l'Anée dernière à Marienbad;* 1961, *Last Year at Marienbad*), he has embodied his idea that the internal reality of consciousness exists in terms of the objects with which it comes in contact. If this is to some extent an idea related to phenomonology, it is also a kind of extreme of materialism. As mentioned earlier, the effects of Robbe-

Grillet are obtained by the omission of psychological development and of such devices as symbol and metaphor —in the last case perhaps less an omission than a reduction, since, with metaphors at least, so many of the adjectives used almost obligatorily are metaphoric in tone or intention. In one passage of *In the Labyrinth*, for example, the snow is described as "un peu plus tassée seulement," which in the English translation becomes "a little more solidly packed," certainly a metaphorical idea; this would apply also to the more usual meaning of the verb (tasser), to heap. Incidentally, that same snow "a cessé à tomber"—"had ceased to fall." And the soldier is described as being "au pied de son réverbère," or "at the foot of his streetlamp," a metaphor, even if, because it has become commonplace, it is the kind known in English as a dead metaphor. Of course Robbe-Grillet cannot escape figurative language altogether, but he does avoid sweeping use of it; he would surely never say, "Ye are the salt of the earth," or "Life's but a walking shadow. . . ."

Further, although Robbe-Grillet attempts to avoid meaning, he cannot altogether do so for, even in his still-life attempts the very objects that he chooses to present suggest a meaning. Why are these particular things projected, and why are they arranged in a certain pattern? By implication, Robbe-Grillet is making a statement about life—his very technique does that, of itself—and he is therefore indulging in philosophy, which deals in meaning. Yet in the commonest use of that word—what does such-and-such *mean?*—Robbe-Grillet is evading the concept, as his characters and situations are left in the mist; unless the reader knows what happens, he cannot properly evaluate the meaning of the story. And with Robbe-Grillet the reader never really knows; the deaths, even murders, of certain characters may not be deaths at all, but fantasies. So here we may have a philosophy ("life exists in terms of objects"; "the events of life are a puzzle") and yet no meaning in the accepted sense, as found in the usual story.

The detractors of Robbe-Grillet have pointed out that

he has diminished the novel by omitting so many of its properties as developed across the centuries, psychology and other adjuncts. But, as indicated earlier, he has helped restore concreteness to a medium that was becoming too abstract; his function has been somewhat similar to that of Cézanne, who at the beginning of this century demonstrated to painters the fundamental shapes of art. And, like some of the successors of Cézanne, Robbe-Grillet finds the "reality" of a work of art in its form: "To speak of the 'content' of a novel simply removes the whole genre from the realm of art. For art contains and expresses nothing. . . . It creates its own equilibrium and its own meaning." If it doesn't stand on its own feet, like the zebra, art falls; and the zebra is real, though its design—its stripes—have no discernible meaning.

In his collected essays, *Pour un Nouveau roman* (1963; *For a New Novel*), Robbe-Grillet defends his method against those who say it lacks humanity. How, he asks, could a book be inhuman, particularly "a novel which deals with a man, and follows his steps from page to page, describing only what he does, what he sees, or what he imagines; how could such a novel be accused of turning away from man?"

For all its novelty, the work of Robbe-Grillet and other practitioners of the nouveau roman seems to some critics to be nothing really fresh; Marcel Thiébaut, for example, has labelled their writings as "not at all a new picture of the world, but the lament or the epic of a suffering neoromantic ego." Chosisme itself is of course not altogether new in that it is an extension of realism and even, in its closeness of observation, of naturalism; and when a critic attacks it as a continuation of romanticism, which it also is, he only reveals his own antiromantic bias. Extensions of the romantic, such as symbolisme and surréalisme, have given modern art some of its most exciting achievements; and those of the chosistes are important among them.

4 *Michel Butor: The Novel as Quest*

Michel Butor speaks of "the novel as quest" in an essay of that name in his *Répertoire* (1960); and most of his fiction has embodied this idea. Butor, who is a teacher, has been connected with schools not only in France, but also in Switzerland, the United States, Greece, and Egypt. His first novel, *Passage de milan* (*Passage of Kites*) appeared in 1954, when its author was twenty-eight.

The kites in the title of the book are the hawks rather ominously observed by the narrator, perhaps as harbingers of doom—since this novel, like so many of those in the nouveau-roman school, contains a murder. This one comes toward the end and is marginal, not really an organic part of the story, which concerns twelve hours (7 P.M. to 7 A.M.) in the lives of a number of persons in a six-story apartment house, ranging from the guests at a party to the concierge on the ground floor to the servants in their narrow rooms under the roof.

In the course of the story, the author projects himself into the consciousness of various characters. He presents scenes that go on simultaneously in different parts of the building, achieving an unusual if often confusing effect of simultaneity. This panoramic story is Butor's largest and most ambitious novel, but it is essentially a tour de force.

Passage of Kites attracted little attention when it came out. Three years later, Butor's third novel, *La Modifica-tion* (1957; *A Change of Heart*; also translated as *Second Thoughts*), brought him a wide public, particularly when the book won the Prix Renaudot. Butor has become the most popular of the nonuveau-roman writers.

His second novel was *l'Emploi du temps* (1956; *Passing Time*), a story set in an English industrial city called Bleston (Butor himself has taught at the University of Manchester). The action reflects the experiences of a young Frenchman, Jacques Revel, who comes to Bleston as a clerk in the firm of Matthews and Sons, exporters, and keeps a journal while there.

The gloomy personality of Bleston is the principal element of the story; it dominates Revel. One of his mechanisms of escape from its dreariness is his weekly visit to a cinéma which conveniently deals in travelogues devoted to far-off and exotic cities. But Revel becomes so enmeshed in Bleston that when he reads a murder mystery set there he sees the story as real and himself as involved in it because of his attempts to discover the facts about an actual death: a local cathedral window devoted to Cain is involved in both the novel Revel reads and the one in which he appears; and, in the novel he reads, a house is described belonging to a man whose brother was killed. Further, the local author who wrote the mystery is nearly run down by a black Morris car; and either this black Morris or another is otherwise an important property in the main story.

There is also a pyromaniac in this town, whose map he burns and, several times, remembers the occasion with relish. Revel becomes the friend of a mysterious, rather sinister Negro and during the course of the story, falls in love with two girls and loses both of them.

Revel had arrived in September, and in May begins his journal, which is both retrospective—describing earlier events with great thoroughness—and of the moment. Revel explains that he writes the diary in order to discover and recover himself, to find out what had really happened to him in "the hated town" with its "wasteland districts," its sooty stations, its rows of brick barracks, its squalor which had tainted his blood and made his head porous so that the very slime of the place could ooze into his skull. Revel and Butor take the reader inside this created city, graphically show its monstrousness. So far, so good—the trouble is, Revel and Butor make the city too opaque, are too occupied with the numbers of bus routes and the names of streets. Most of the latter are stodgily British and merely add density; occasionally one of the imagined names has a certain effectiveness, such as the Slee, a

wonderfully sinister designation for the river that slides
through the town. But Butor's overspecific emphasis on
nonexistent streets and hotels and numbered districts
becomes tiring. On the other hand, Butor's contemporary,
Robbe-Grillet, far more persuasively projects a city in *In
the Labyrinth*, using suggestiveness rather than all the
denotation that hampers the narrative in Butor's *Passing
Time*.

Unlike Robbe-Grillet, however, Butor doesn't consciously avoid figurative language. His book is full of it:
shadows creep, sunbeams are nimble fingered, certain
events blind the narrator, a cathedral is the huge skeleton
of a whale—and so on. And when Butor isn't too tangled
up in street names and numbers of the districts of the
town, he achieves some fine effects of evocation. The book
is essentially a mystery and remains a mystery to the last:
at the end of his journal, Revel say that an event of
February 29 which he had forgotten to set down, and now
doesn't have time to do so, was very important. Perhaps it
would have presented a key to the whole story.

A Change of Heart—which, as noted earlier, was
Michel Butor's third novel, a prize winner published in
1957 as *La Modification*—is not a mystery except that all
these antinovels deal in the mystery of personality. But
what happens in *A Change of Heart* is fairly easy to
discover. Indeed, the central line of action is quite simple;
the interest in the story lies in the application of its
method.

This is an approach to the subject through the second-
person view; that is, the narrator, in the stream of
consciousness that comprises the whole story, continually
addresses himself as "you." This is not an improbability, is
in no way unreal, yet stretched through a book it doesn't
have the force of the second-person approach supposed to
be so effective in advertisements, which are of course
shorter.

The entire story takes place, as noted, in the narrator's
consciousness; the outward setting is a railway compartment on a trip between Paris and Rome. Léon, Paris

manager for an Italian typewriter manufacturer, decides to leave his boring wife, Henriette, for his mistress in Rome, Cécile. Léon plans to tell Cécile of his decision at the end of the journey, but before it is over he undergoes a modification, a change of heart, so that by the time the train arrives in Rome he has decided not to abandon his wife. The story itself is as easy as all that, embellished during Léon's long monologue by memories of both women, of the Paris apartment and of the Roman scenery of which Cécile is so much a part—so much, indeed, that when Léon remembers her visit to Paris, he recalls that she didn't have about her the glamour with which Rome invests her.

A *Change of Heart* is clever rather than profound. Michel Butor discovered an unusually apt setting for the second-person unreeling of Léon's stream of consciousness, for the whirling background of a rail journey strikes the mind with images and associations, driving the memory inward; and this is neatly conveyed by Butor, even though the method at the last becomes a little wearisome, most of all perhaps because his observation is often conventional and commonplace, and his writing altogether less intense than that of Nathalie Sarraute and Alain Robbe-Grillet.

In *Degrés* (1960; *Degrees*), Michel Butor tells a story through the mirrors of indirecton. It deals with an October day in the life of a lycée professor who teaches history and geography, and the trouble that besets him. Pierre Vernier attempts to catch the reality of his environment, with all its ramifications in the life of his students and fellow teachers and their families. The attempt is to be made, Vernier tells himself, for the sake of his nephew, a student in the school, who as a result of Vernier's documentation will have an important segment of his life preserved. Vernier's trouble comes from the strain of trying to catch and fix reality. Feeling that he must extend his point of view beyond himself, Vernier in his manuscript pretends that he also is the recording consciousness of one of his colleagues as well as of his nephew himself.

The degrees of the title convey the idea of all these complicated interrelationships, set against the background of Vernier's history lessons dealing with the Classic and French heroic periods, which further intensify the idea of degrees.

Vernier's excessive exploration of what might be called daily-ness stretches his mind too far; he has in effect violated what most people think of as reality. He ends in the hospital.

During the course of the story, Butor has provided the reader not only with the events of the classroom, and the impingement of past events upon them, but also with the intricacies of the lives of Vernier's colleagues and of his own love affair with Micheline Pavin. *Degrees* is a microscopic investigation of the life processes themselves, more detailed even than the explorations of Sarraute and Robbe-Grillet, with fewer clues as to what is happening. It is therefore somewhat more difficult to read, but the book remains a fascinating experiment; it deals more thoroughly with space-time concepts than other novels of its school.

The tendency toward flatness in Butor's writing is apparent in *Mobile* (1962), an account of his trip across the United States. The book is a tiresome montage of disconnected images relieved by catalogues of names, advertising slogans, the prose of road signs. A poor imitation of the expressionist techniques, *Mobile* never brings the reader inside the material, as *Passing Time* so often does, making him a participant in the gloomy horror of Bleston. But *Mobile* instead represents a deterioration of the method that sometimes made A *Change of Heart* a vivid travelogue.

Butor's American experiences have also induced him to write a novel, *6,810,000 Litres of Water Per Second* (1965), a story in which Niagara Falls are thunderously dominant. The action, chiefly concerned with newly married couples and older ones nostalgically returning, covers a year, presenting events somewhat in the manner of *Mobile*, with different kinds of type and with speeches intended to be read at different pitches. The tricks tend to overpower the story and to make the reader long for the Butor who once excitingly dramatized an international train-journey and who once made a dull English industrial seem interesting. While Alain Robbe-Grillet has advanced the technique of the new novel, Michel Butor has increasingly resorted to mere tricks. But his notable achievements of the past remain.

5 *Other Antinovel Novelists*

The nouveau-roman group became, in the space of a few years, a fairly large one. Among its members who have not so far been mentioned, critics and other readers have various favorites. These remaining members of the school, exclusive of Beckett—whose affiliations with it are doubtful—will now be discussed in a generally chronological order, except in the case of Hélène Bessette, whose birth date has not been made available. Her works include *Lilli pleure* (1953; *Lilli Weeps*), *Les Petites Lecocq* (1955; *The Little Lecocqs*), *La Tour* (1959; *The Tower*), *La Route bleue* (1960; *The Blue Route*), *N'avez-vous pas froid?* (1963; *Aren't You Cold?*), and *Si j'étais vous* (1963; *If I Were You*). Hélène Bessette's novels have the spasmodic, cinematic quality of most of the other antiroman writers, but her work seems more superficial and less organized. Further, its total effect is one of choppiness, since she frequently uses incomplete sentences.

The name of Marguerite Duras, born in 1914 and brought up in Indochina, became familiar across the world in 1959 as the writer of the screenplay and dialogue for the Alain Resnais film, *Hiroshima mon amour*. Here, the abrupt transitions, the clipped angles, and the intensive focus on objects created interesting photographic effects out of the technical devices of the antinovel, shading in this case into chosisme. Earlier, the filming of one of her novels had helped make her name known; this was her third book, *Un Barrage contre le pacifique* (1950;

The Sea Wall), set in Indochina and called *This Angry Age* on the screen. It is the story of a young man and his sister, and the disorder which arises when Joseph discovers passion. Mlle. Duras, who studied mathematics, political science, and law (licenses in the last two) at the Sorbonne, had earlier written *Les Impudents* (1943; *The Shameless*) and *La Vie tranquille* (1944; *The Quiet Life*). The latter, whose locale is a southwestern farm, projects an intense family story, centering on a young peasant who kills his uncle and subsequently kills himself; the story is told in the first person by his sister Françou, herself entangled in a love affair with a young farmer. The characters are deliberately dehumanized, shown as only half alive.

Marguerite Duras's later novels include: *Le Marin de Gibraltar* (1952; *The Sailor from Gibraltar*), *Le Square* (1955; *The Square*), *Moderato Cantabile* (1958), *Dix Heures et demie du soir en été* (1960; *Ten-Thirty on a Summer Night*), and *l'Après-midi de Monsieur Andesmas* (1962; *The Afternoon of Monsieur Andesmas*). In *The Sailor from Gibraltar*, Anne seeks across the world for a sailor from that place, joined in her quest by a man who remains nameless, who in order to go with Anne leaves a woman with whom he has been existing in an indifferent, half-alive way. *The Square* is made up almost entirely of dialogue, the conversation of two people. A housemaid of twenty, supervising a child in the park, falls into talk with a traveling salesman—talk that is trivial at first but that slowly grows into something momentous for them both, a promised end of loneliness as the conclusion of the story suggests further meetings. *Moderato Cantabile* and *Ten-Thirty on a Summer Night* are more overtly dramatic. In *Moderato Cantabile*, the background is projected in terms of the title: a child misunderstood by his mother takes daily piano lessons next to a café where she sits drinking. Once she witnesses a murder, a man strangling the woman he loves. The witness, Anne Desbaresdes, the wife of a wealthy manufacturer, is haunted by the vision of the murderer kissing the bloody mouth of the woman he has killed. Anne keeps returning to the café, carrying on an elaborate dialogue with a worker she meets there, Chauvin, and the two of them continually play out the murder scene in their talk; they recognize the possibility that Anne is a type to be murdered and Chauvin a type to commit a murder. When Chauvin says, "I wish that you were dead," Anne replies, "It is done."

The setting of *Ten-Thirty on a Summer Night* is a small town in Spain; the story begins in a damp café, with lighted candles and occasional rain. The alcoholic Maria, on a trip with her husband and child and a woman friend, Claire, hears of one Rodrigo Paestra, who has killed his young wife and her lover and has disappeared; she feels an intense sympathy for him. At night, Maria is on a hotel balcony and sees, when lightning flares, her husband and Claire embracing, a flight above. At the same moment, Maria glimpses the murderer hiding on a nearby rooftop. She helps him to escape, but he kills himself in a field. As the travelers continue their trip, Maria goes on drinking and waits for the time when her husband and Claire will openly become lovers. The situation is intensified by the atmosphere, the heat and dampness of Spain, the sensual quality of the food and wine. Of all the nouveau-roman writers, Marguerite Duras is the one most concerned with sex, its oppressiveness and its force.

In *The Afternoon of Monsieur Andesmas*, Mme. Duras tells an almost immobile story of an almost immobile man. During an entire afternoon, Monsieur Andesmas, who is in his late seventies, sits before his house and rarely lifts his massive bulk from the wicker chair in which he awaits his daughter. Valérie, who is seventeen, delays her arrival; so does Michel Arc, a builder who has been engaged to make a terrace in front of that house, purchased for Valérie by her doting father. As Monsieur Andesmas waits, he is informed by Michel Arc's wife that her husband and Valérie have become lovers. But there is no dramatic confrontation; the afternoon fades, Michel Arc and Valérie do not appear, and Monsieur Andesmas waits on for them in his creaking wicker chair.

Despite the lack of eventful outer action, however, a

great deal has happened; the life of Monsieur Andesmas has drastically changed. And the author projects a living landscape: the white house, the small valley below it which is "a chasm of light," the surrounding trees. There are stories in which there is more landscape than human action in the usual sense—Hemingway's "Big Two-Hearted River" is an example of a somewhat different kind—stories in which the landscape is dominant. This applies to the account of Monsieur Andesmas, whose afternoon is looked back upon from a point in the future —he survived the crisis—a point from which the natural surroundings appear as the important thing in the story. Marguerite Duras has presented them with effective intensity.

Like Marguerite Duras, Claude Mauriac was born in 1914. Son of the novelist François Mauriac, Claude Mauriac became a critic of films and literature before turning to the novel. In 1958, his *l'Alittérature contemporaine*, which has been translated as *The New Literature*, became one of the great rallying cries of the nouveau-roman and antinovel group. He had made his début as a novelist in 1957 with *Toutes les Femmes sont fatales* (*All Women are Fatal*), the story of the youthful love affairs of Bertrand Carnéjoux, in Rio de Janeiro, New York, and Paris: it is a chronicle of eroticism, played out entirely in Bertrand's consciousness.

It was two years later that Claude Mauriac attracted wide attention with a novel, *Le Dîner en ville* (1959; *The Dinner Party*). He followed this with *La Marquise sortit à cinq heures* (1961; *The Marquise Went Out at Five*). These are important contributions to alittérature. In each of these novels, as in so many antinovel novels, a map is provided at the beginning of the book. In *The Dinner Party*, the map shows the seating arrangement, so that the reader may trace the streams of thought that emanate from the various characters. In *The Marquise Went Out at Five*, the plan shows the Carrefour de Buci, in the Saint-Germain-des-Prés section of Paris, in which the story takes place.

In *The Dinner Party*, the setting is an apartment on the

Île Saint-Louis, with views of the Seine after dark, and Notre-Dame lighted up; there is a soft fall of rain, and now and then an illuminated bateau-mouche passes on the river. The host at the dinner party is Bertrand Carnéjoux, now a middle-aged man, successful at writing and with women; his young wife, Martine, familiarly known as Pilou, during the dinner almost drifts into a love affair with one of the guests, but stops when she remembers her children, whom at the end of the dinner she slips off to see for a moment while they are sleeping. The Carnéjoux serve champagne with every course, so that they and their six guests are highly stimulated. The guests are a mixed lot, including an ancient and faded beauty; a young man who grew up with the hostess; the screenwriter to whom the hostess is attracted; a young model from Canada who believes that her love affair with the host will help her acting career; a wealthy bachelor who broods over his impotence, and a sun-tanned woman in her forties who, in the middle of the party, is recognized by the host as a girl from the provinces with whom he had had a love affair twenty years before.

The conversation bubbles, but underneath it the thoughts of the eight characters are reflected as these thoughts go counterclockwise around the table. The talk is trivial, often literary, but the thoughts are concerned with elemental matters, love and death, and each of the characters undergoes some significant change during the dinner.

In Claude Mauriac's *The New Literature*, he speaks of Paul Valéry as one who scorned the novel, chiefly for its imprecision, though he was, as Mauriac points out, one of the forerunners of the alittérature school. Valéry once said that he could never write a novel because he could never write down the commonplace narrative notations that make up such productions. Mauriac was in effect accepting the challenge Valéry had left when he took for a title the very phrase Valéry mentioned as being the sort of thing he could not write: *The Marquise Went Out at Five*. In this book, Mauriac again introduces Bertrand

Carnéjoux, now separated from Martine and no longer living on the Île Saint-Louis but in an apartment off the Carrefour de Buci, whose throngs of people Bertrand watches from his window as Claude Mauriac unfolds below him the whole teeming life of the area, its movement and its sounds. Again the author shifts from one of his characters to the other, revealing that character's thoughts and impressions, this time even introducing parts of the surging past of the carrefour. One of the people involved in the present is the plump figure Zerbanian, somewhat remotely introduced in the earlier novel, the middle-aged homosexual who had telephoned to Martine his regrets at not being able to attend her dinner party. The later book begins, "The Marquise went out at five." But did she (or he)? The last sentence in the book seems to deny it. Mauriac does little to clear up the mystery in his subsequent book, *l'Agrandissement* (1963; *The Enlargement*), which deals with some of the same people.

Somewhat older than Claude Mauriac, Maurice Blanchot (born 1907), a distinguished critic, is perhaps the most difficult to read of all the nouveau-roman writers. He is in a sense a forerunner, with *Thomas l'obscur* (1941; *Thomas the Obscure*). In this book, Thomas frustratedly seeks out different identifications in a setting which sometimes seems real enough—a coastal area—as does Thomas' fiancée, Anne, who seems involved in the story; but much of it is hallucination. Blanchot in his later work becomes increasingly obscure, as in *Le Très-Haut* (1948; *The Most High*). Blanchot has been compared to the James Joyce of *Finnegans Wake*, to Franz Kafka and, perhaps more accurately, to Stéphane Mallarmé.

Jean Cayrol, born in 1911, is considerably easier to follow, although his work sometimes becomes lost in a poetic mist. Cayrol, who frequently uses the figure of Lazarus as a symbol, published two volumes of somewhat surréaliste poetry before the Second World War, during three years of which he was a prisoner in a concentration camp because of résistance activities. He has since the war continued to write poetry, but began as a novelist with the trilogy *Je vivrai l'amour des autres* (1947–50; *I Shall Live the Love of Others*). This consists of *On vous parle* (1947; *One Speaks to You*), *Les Premiers Jours* (1947; *The First Days*), and *Le Feu qui prend* (1950; *The Fire That Seizes*); the first two volumes won the Prix Théophraste Renaudot in 1947. *One Speaks to You* is the monologue of a vagrant named Armand, who has been in a concentration camp and now drifts through a city vaguely ruminating his past; he is an example of what Cayrol has called the Lazare parmi nous, the Lazarus among us, back from the dead and living in his own world, without human contact. In the second volume, *The First Days*, Armand is seen from without, in a third-person narrative. The book, notable for its elongated dream sequence, shows Armand coming to life and into identification with humanity through his growing love for Lucette. In *The Fire That Seizes*, Armand, who has gone home to visit his mother, meets Francine, whose face has "a secret radiance." Lucette, with whom he has broken, seeks him out after she has been fatally wounded; as she dies in a hospital, Armand and Francine—who has also been away, in the clutches of a religious sect—realize that their lives are joined together forever, and that in this union they will attain their highest humanity. Cayrol, a deeply believing Catholic, expresses with intensity his religious exaltation, though without the fervent evangelic melodrama of Georges Bernanos. In *La Noire* (1949; *The Black*), Cayrol tells two stories, one the objective love story of the girl Armande and the lover she calls Tristan, the other a monologue of a man who seems to be making up the story against the background of war and a ruined world; after this nameless monologist says that Armande has died, he announces that he will then marry Armande's mean-spirited sister who may, despite her cruelty, become one day "a rediscovered Armande."

Cayrol's *Le Vent de la mémoire* (1952; *The Wind of Memory*) lives up to its title by presenting the storm of memories which occur to the writer Gérard, full of self-reproach for his own viciousness and his inability to love, but there is some hope for his becoming humanized through the love of a young woman who accepts him as he is. Cayrol, who doesn't indulge in religious propaganda, nevertheless deeply explores the dilemma of human beings in the secular world of today. In *l'Éspace d'une nuit* (1954; *The Space of a Night*) François returns to his native town on his thirtieth birthday in response to an ambiguous message he has received in Paris. Getting off the train before it has reached the town, where his cruel and overbearing father lives, François wanders through the space of night, freeing himself from the lifelong domination of his now dying father and discovering a new identity, maturity itself, which is signalized by the rise of dawn. Daybreak also plays an important role in *Le Déménagement* (1956; *The Removal*), in which the light after darkness suggests that a woman who, with her immediate family and later her husband, has been icily inhuman and unloving, will attempt to change her life.

The long story, *La Gaffe* (1957; *The Blunder*), is set in the foggy atmosphere of a coast town in Brittany, where the central character, who has just broken with his mistress, struggles with his despair and with the realization that he can't restore the relationship. Gaspard in *Les Corps étrangers* (1959; *Foreign Bodies*) presents an endless and repetitive story of his life, mixing what may be true with what seems false; Gaspard came to the city from a farm, took part in the black market during the war, has been a thief, pimp, and possibly a murderer, yet through this tangled confessional he seems to move from anguish toward hope. The novels of Cayrol are profound explorations, but their outlines are too often blurred by the incessant poetry which prevents the definition not only of character but of occurrence and theme; atmospherically, however, the books are rich.

Born of French parents in Madagascar in 1913, Claude Simon learned much from both Albert Camus and William Faulkner. His first novel, *Le Tricheur* (1945; *The Trickster*), is very much in the vein of Camus's *The*

Stranger. By the time he had reached his fifth novel, *Le Vent* (1957; *The Wind*), Simon was using Faulkner-like thousand-word sentences and elongated parentheses. But, like Faulkner, Simon by means of such methods often achieves impressive effects; the wind of his story, for example, is supremely orchestrated, the wind blowing across the vineyards over which Simon's central character, the saintly simple Antoine Montès, wanders. *L'Herbe* (1958; *The Grass*) is even more poetic, and the story plays a more important part in the book this time, as a group of characters look back on their lives, which once covered the earth like the blowing grass. But they are unaware of it; Simon puts at the front of his book a quotation from Boris Pasternak, "No one makes the story; one does not see it any more than he sees the grass growing." And in the book one of the characters uses the word endurer, to endure, speaking of the necessity to do so, which is reminiscent of what Faulkner said about Dilsey and his other Negro characters: "They endured."

In *La Route des Flandres* (1960; *The Flanders Road*), Simon seems more the follower of Conrad and Proust than of Faulkner, though by this time he has developed a vision distinctly his own. In this novel he presents a kaleidoscopic account of the fall of France in 1940, in a mixture of narration and stream of consciousness. The jerky, violent, many-colored interior monologues that make up the book are an excellent mode of presentation for the effect upon several soldiers of that 1940 collapse. Simon uses the stream-of-consciousness technique not for psychological exploration, but rather for the projection of experience itself, in a manner at once piercing and solid. The figure that dominates the story is an aristocratic officer, Captain de Reixach, who is killed in battle, after which he and the properties of his existence are reconstructed by three of his soldiers who wander through France and in and out of prison camps. There are some extremely detailed erotic passages, ideally suited to the interior-monologue method which, elliptical and lyrical, gives them an effective embodiment as it follows what is fluid and what is fixed in human experience.

In *Le Pire* (1954; *The Worst*), by Jean Lagrolet (born 1918), the people of a small kingdom learn from their dying monarch that God doesn't exist, hence didn't support the régime. The succeeding king, watching his subjects struggle for power over what is left, establishes an arbitrary rule, after which the author offers some reflections about arbitrariness. In *Les Vainqueurs du Jaloux* (1957; *The Conquerors of the Jealous One*), Lagrolet is, in the compulsive dialogues, somewhat near the technique of Nathalie Sarraute; in this first-person story, told by a man named Gilles, Lagrolet lets the characters, chiefly members of a luncheon party at the country house of Gilles's neighbor, reveal themselves largely through conversation, or actually don't reveal themselves, since their talk is essentially a mask, wild enough at times, and interesting in a rather frenzied way, but concealing depths of mystery. Robert Pinget, born in Geneva in 1920, showed in his early works a tendency toward mischievous fantasy, in such books as *Entre Fantoine et Agapa* (1950; *Between Fantoine and Agapa*) and *Graal flibuste* (1956; *Filibustering Grail*), the latter set in a strange kingdom where odd animals exist, including the butterfly-monkeys, the poppy-dogs, and the bird-tigers. Pinget distinctly showed that he had much in common with the new-novel, antinovel group in *Le Fiston* (1958; *Sonny*, translated as *Monsieur Levert*). In this, a father spends his nights composing a long, confused letter to his son, a chronicle in which the events that occur in the town are jumbled in with the father-son relationship. Pinget dramatized this novel as *Lettre morte* (*Dead Letter*) for the Salle Récamier to present during the 1959–60 season. *Clope au dossier* (1961; *Clope with the Dossier*) is the narrative version of *La Manivelle* (*The Crank*), which Samuel Beckett translated and adapted for BBC. In *Clope*, a madman defending himself puts together a dossier which includes, like *Sonny*, all the clattering life of a French town.

Claude Ollier, born 1922, has written against the background of his North African experiences in *La Mise en scène* (1958; *The Setting*) and *Le Maintien de l'ordre*

(1961; *The Maintenance of Order*). In the first book, an engineer named Lassalle, mapping a road across the desert to a mining settlement, is mystified by traces of a predecessor; in the second, gunmen follow a man through a city. Ollier, a disciple of Alain Robbe-Grillet, concentrates intensely on the object. North Africa is also the setting of the novel *Nedjma* (1956), by Kateb Yacine, who was born in 1929 near Constantine, Algeria; Yacine means writer in Arabic. *Nedjma*, written in French, is a complicatedly woven story of a magnetic girl, half-French and half-native, who seems a symbol of Algeria itself. The story telescopes time, not only in Arab fashion, seeing it as circular rather than linear, but very much in the manner of the new-novel writers, to whose literature Kateb Yacine has made an exotic and interesting contribution.

Enough has been said in the foregoing to indicate what the antiliterature novelists are doing. And although they are often criticized for being full of tricks, or too preoccupied with technique, they have nevertheless accounted for some significant creations. In France at least they have attracted a wide public which admires the very excellence of their stylistic accomplishment and will no longer accept flaccid or sloppy writing. The contribution of the antinovelists, when assimilated as both influence and achievement, can be regarded only as progressive. It has the potential of leading the novel forward.

6 THE LITERATURE OF THE ABSURD

1 *The Geography of the Absurd*

Absurdity, which is one of the existentialiste concepts, has been turned to various literary uses, some of them primarily existential, some of them not. There is no definite school of absurdity, with members and regulations—but there are a number of writers who have this quality in common, chiefly dramatists—and to mention several of them together is not to suggest that they form a group except in the largest sense. Their novels and plays certainly have a common ancestry in various phases of modernism: in futurisme, cubisme, dadaïsme, and surréalisme, as well as in the works of such men as Franz Kafka. But a good deal of comedy, especially parody, lies in the background, too, from parts of Aristophanes (though not his fundamental political thinking), through the Commedia dell'arte, Edward Lear and Lewis Carroll, vaudeville, and the Keystone cops. It is in our own time that the absurd often becomes serious, at times even suggesting the contours of new forms of tragedy.

The absurd has always confronted man, but perhaps never so much as today when he seems to have virtually everything within his grasp and may lose the grasp itself. Life consistently invents its own scenarios of absurdity.

Paris is the center of absurd literature, for not only do native practitioners of the absurd such as Jean Genet live there, but also Arthur Adamov, born in Russia; Fernando Arrabal, a native of what was Spanish Morocco; Samuel Beckett, from Dublin, and Eugène Ionesco, who came out of Rumania.

2 "Saint Genet": Perhaps More Villon than Villain

Biographically, the most spectacular author of the twentieth century is Jean Genet. His novels and plays are hardly less spectacular.

Born in Paris, apparently in 1910, Jean Genet didn't know who his father was. Abandoned by his mother, Genet was sent first to an orphanage and then to a Burgundian peasant family. Caught stealing at the age of ten, he was put into a reformatory, the first of many such sentences. To Jean-Paul Sartre, Genet at this time made his existential choice: accused of being a thief, he decided to be a thief, "converted, illumined, confirmed. Impossible to reverse direction." When he was old enough Genet joined the French Foreign Legion, from which he deserted. Wandering across Europe in the 1930's, he was a thief, beggar, and male prostitute, learning every corner of the underworld and inhabiting the cells of many prisons. While in one of them during the Second World War, he began writing a novel on the brown paper from which convicts were supposed to make bags. One of his jailors saw the manuscript, took it away, and burned it. Genet started his novel again. As Sartre says in his remarkable, brilliant, and searching book, *Saint Genet: comédien et martyr* (1952; *Saint Genet: Actor and Martyr*), "Nothing in the world mattered to him but those pieces of brown paper that a match could reduce to ashes." In this way Genet wrote *Notre-Dame des fleurs* (*Our Lady of the Flowers*), miraculously issued in a limited edition in Lyon in 1943 (revised edition, Paris 1951). It is an epic of the homosexual underground. And, since the solitary author in Fresnes prison often used the Aladdin's lamp of onanism, Sartre says that the book is "the epic of masturbation."

The narrator, in Cell 426, cuts pictures out of magazines and with a fine irony—since they are pictures of criminals —pastes them on the back of the sheet of prison regulations on his wall. He weaves fantasies around the pictures, reconstructing the trial of the young murderer known as Our Lady of the Flowers, who at sixteen strangled an old man, just as an acte gratuit. But most of the book hovers about Louis Culafroy, the male prostitute known in the Pigalle area of Paris as Divine [Mignon]. Divine dies of tuberculosis during the story, vomiting blood. Besides Divine, there is also a bizarre gallery of homoerotics, with their fancy English hats, fake jewelry, and pointed yellow shoes, a gallery including Divine's erotic partner who also acts as "her" pimp, one Darling, whom Mimosa the Second steals from Divine. But Divine has a Negro friend, Seck Gorgui, alias the Archangel Gabriel, who has killed his mistress. In résumé all this takes on a false simplicity that in no way does justice to the complexity, force, delicacy, and beauty of the original. Genet has, along with his other writing achievements, one of the finest prose styles, if not the very finest, in twentieth-century French writing. As for Genet's evocation of the dark aspects of life, Jean-Paul Sartre has pointed out that although French literature is generally known, outside France, for its humanism and rationalism, it has always produced "works that are secret and black," which may well be "its most beautiful creations." Sartre mentions François Villon, the Marquis de Sade, Arthur Rimbaud, and the Count de Lautréamont: "It may well be that Genet, latest of such magicians, is also the greatest of them."

The inspiration for *Our Lady of the Flowers*, to whose memory the book is dedicated, was Roger Pilorge, "whose death continues to plague my life." Genet met him in prison "'His body and his radiant face haunt my nights without sleep." Genet, escorted by a turnkey, used to bring Pilorge a cigarette every morning in his death-cell, and Pilorge with a smile would greet him, "Hail, Jean of the morning." Pilorge, who killed his lover Escudero for less than a thousand francs, went to the guillotine at Saint-Brieuc in March, 1939. In writing of Pilorge, Genet has spoken of "the double and unique splendor of his soul and body." It was to Pilorge that Genet also wrote his famous poem, "Le Condamné à mort" ("The Man Condemned to Death"), which begins:

> *The wind that rolls a heart on the courtyard pavings*
> *An angel that weeps caught in a tree*
> *The azure column round which the marble twines*
> *Open in my night emergency exits.*

Miracle de la rose (1943; *Miracle of the Rose*), written in La Santé and Tourelles prisons, begins with the narrator going to jail. Then he starts to speak of his love affairs, particularly the one with Bulkaen, who is coy and before whom the narrator hopes not to betray himself by too much eagerness. But Bulkaen, in whom the reader is becoming interested, proves to be a young man; as Sartre says, Genet "has played his finest trick on decent folk." But much of the book is a praise of burglary, really a poetics of it, and the story ends with a litany of criminals' names that surges into poetry.

Pompes funèbres (1945; *Funeral Rites*) deals with a lover of Genet's who was killed as a member of the résistance. The book is one of the great stories of the German occupation, with the Nazi military man Erik as one of the chief characters, and even Hitler evoked from time to time. The tortuous love affairs accentuate the confused atmosphere of the time, and the people and places are presented under the spell of Genet's poetic magic.

In *Querelle de Brest* (1946), Genet's hero is the sailor Querelle, a murderer who is flagrantly amoral. He engages in a love affair with the very detective who is trying to solve one of the murders Querelle has committed. This book, full of the foggy dockside area of Brest, Genet left unfinished: "The onset of boredom made us give up *Querelle*, which already was starting to peter out." But the force of the book remains.

Embodying the relationship which Thomas Mann always envisioned between criminal and artist, Genet after he became a recognized writer did not stop his burglaries and, upon receiving his tenth condemnation, was by law sentenced to life imprisonment. But France's literary world rose to his defense: Sartre, Jean Cocteau and others petitioned the president of France, and the sentence was remitted. In 1949, Genet brought out *Journal du voleur* (*The Thief's Journal*), with its cry from the heart of the convict in his cell. "O let me be only beauty! I will go quickly or slowly, but will dare what has to be dared. I will shatter appearances, the casings will be burned away and will fall off me, and I shall appear, one evening, on the palm of your hand, calm and pure as a glass statuette." The story is set in the 1930's, in the underworld of Barcelona, with occasional flashes of the back streets of other cities, in France, Poland, Germany, and Czechoslovakia. Genet writes of the vermin crawling over Spain. "I was conscious of being a louse"—but there is always in the reader's mind that heart-deep cry for beauty. Sartre calls *The Thief's Journal* Genet's most beautiful book, and "the *Dichtung und Warheit* of homosexuality."

Genet has achieved his greatest fame in the theater. *Les Bonnes* (1947; *The Maids*), first staged by Louis Jouvet at the Athenée, deals with relationship between two maids, the sisters Claire and Solange, and their mistress, Madame. A fourth character, who never appears, Monsieur, casts a shadow across the action. Genet wanted the three women to be played by adolescent boys, but Jouvet, who put up with the themes of lesbianism, sadism, and murder in the drama, insisted upon having actresses. Sartre defends Genet's wish to have boys in the rôles, not just because boys please Genet but because they would heighten the artificiality not only of a theatrical performance, but of this one especially, because it is essentially a drama of disguises. As the curtain rises, one of the maids is dressing Madame, who eventually turns out not to be Madame at all, but Claire getting into Madame's clothes and imitating her gestures before her dressing-table. Ultimately, planning to murder her mistress, Claire's identification with her goes so far that she drinks the poison herself. With the love-hate relationship existing among the principals (though Madame treats Claire and Solange kindly), the flagellation, the mock murder that turns into an actual death, the play is one of almost unrelieved horror, surely one of the most brutally effective dramas of the time.

Genet himself staged *Haute Surveillance* (1949; *Death-watch*) at the Théâtre des Mathurins. The scene is a prison cell inhabited by three young men: Yeux-verts (Green Eyes), Lefranc, and Maurice. Green Eyes, awaiting the guillotine for the murder of a young girl, exalts his crime and dominates Maurice, who in turn lords it over Lefranc. Behind the action the audience can feel the presence of an important character who never appears: the Negro criminal Boule-de-Neige (Snowball). The lust of sex, power, and murder flourish in the play, which ends with a spectacular crime.

Le Balcon (1957; *The Balcony*) can, however, give spectators an even sharper jab of shock. Genet strips away the mask of society itself. The first performance of the play was in London, for members of the Arts Theater Club whose private productions are beyond the reach of the Lord Chamberlain, who would hardly have appreciated the characterization of high officials in the play. *The Balcony* was put on in Paris at the Théâtre du Gymnase in 1960, and shortly after it began jarring New York audiences in a theater-in-the-round production at Greenwich Village's Circle in the Square (in a vigorously fine translation by Bernard Frechtman, who has done much toward conveying the essence of Genet's plays and novels in English). In *The Balcony*, the audience receives its first jolt when it discovers that the robed bishop uttering theological ideas is not in an ecclesiastical palace but in an elaborate brothel whose proprietress, Irma, has a periscope system that allows her to see into every room. The bishop is only a petty worker for the gas company. Similarly, the bewigged judge flogging the girl delinquent is also only a small-time citizen, and so is the man who swaggers about in a general's uniform which is one of the costumes that can be rented from Madame Irma.

Ironically, while these creatures are indulging their erotic fantasies, the world outside the brothel is shaking with revolution, whose sounds occasionally penetrate. The queen and her principal functionaries are killed when the royal palace is blown up, after which an official invites Madame Irma to become queen and the false bishop, judge, and general to step into these positions in actuality. They of course become bored with reality: playing the rôles was so much more fun. But all is well when a new revolution sends "Queen" Irma back to her brothel, and Genet's wry comment on modern society achieves its gross and grotesque climax. In one episode which can hardly be characterized as anything but unforgettable, one of the characters on the stage castrates himself.

Les Nègres (1959; *The Blacks*), was originally directed by Roger Blin at the Lutèce, with the group of Negro actors known as Les Griots. The play has no plot in the usual sense, since it is essentially a ritual enacted by a crowd of Negroes, supposedly the sacrificial murder of a white woman. A group of Negroes who remain in the background supposedly represent various phases of white colonialism, including queen, missionary, governor, and judge, who are all later "murdered" also. Genet has put forward no plea for an end of racism, or for better treatment of Negroes, but rather has projected, in what he calls a clownerie (clownplay), an elaboration of Negro fantasies about white people. It is a grotesque anthropological fantasy which makes white audiences uncomfortable but succeeds in magnetizing them into the theater.

Genet's *Les Paravents* (1961; *The Screens*) was forbidden performance in France because of sensitivity over Algeria. It was first played in Berlin. The drama takes its name from the screens, about ten feet high with landscapes and various objects painted on them, rolled back and forth during the play's seventeen scenes. The stage directions call for the actors to wear masks, or to be made up excessively, often with false noses, even with false chins. The acting should be "extremely precise" and "very taut," with "no useless gestures"; and what gestures are used should be "*visible*." Since the cast contains nearly a hundred characters, Genet suggests that each actor play several parts. The principal rôle is that of Saïd, an Arab so poor that he can marry only the homeliest girl. The play introduces many phases of Algerian society, including of course a brothel, as well as fields, houses, a marketplace, a barracks, an orange grove and other appropriate settings, with the action sometimes occurring on several levels at once. Sex has its usual emphasis, indeed here more extremely than in other Genet plays, but *The Screens* lacks the theatrical force of *The Maids* or *The Balcony*. None of his plays is helped by dramatic form, but *The Maids* and *The Balcony* have an intensity the others lack.

Sartre called his book about this writer *Saint Genet* because of St. Genestus (in French, Genest or Genêt), the Roman actor and martyr of the third century who became the patron saint of players, and the hero of Jean de Rotrou's seventeenth-century tragedy, *Le véritable Saint Genest*. The "black-magic" aspect of Jean Genet, to many who have followed his plays and novels, is ritualistic, exalting (however debasing), and holy (however invertedly so). Despite his often implicit social criticisms, which tend to suggest that he is at the edge of being a propagandist, and despite existential elements in his works and statements, with their occasional commitment, Genet remains one of the powerful contributors to the literature of the absurd.

3 *The Antitheater of Ionesco*

In discussing Samuel Beckett, the *New Republic's* drama critic Robert Brustein mentioned Eugène Ionesco: Beckett, "like Ionesco, has so successfully persuaded us of the validity, coherence, and theatrical relevance of this vision [of existence] that we are impatient when he repeats the lesson. Ionesco's recent work has exposed his severe limitations, and I doubt if he will ever be much more than a stunning secondary dramatist," unlike Beckett, whose work has "superior power, beauty, and intelligence."

The chief limitation of Ionesco, about which many critics agree, is his failure of growth, partly because of the inability of the absurd to be extensive. Yet, within these handicaps, Ionesco has occasionally provided some interesting theater.

Born in France in 1912, Ionesco lived there for the first thirteen years of his life. After this he was taken to his father's native Rumania, where he spent the next fourteen. He became a teacher of French there, but disliked the national tendency toward fascism, as exemplified by the Iron Guard. He returned to France in 1938 and has lived there ever since.

According to his own statement, Ionesco became a playwright by accident. In 1948, while attempting to learn a third language—English—Ionesco bought a phrase manual which reproduced the conversation of two couples, the Smiths and the Martins. What they said, he has reported, was mechanistic Cartesian logic: the week has seven days, the floor is beneath us, ceiling is over us, and so on; these were indisuptable truths Ionesco had long since forgotten, or merely taken for granted, and suddenly these statements began to seem not only fundamental but profound. He was driven to put these commonplaces into the dialogue of a play in which the Martins call on the Smiths. Ionesco of course gave it a deliberately ridiculous framework (and then pretended surprise when audiences laughed) by beginning the play with the clock striking seventeen. And even the title he gave to the play, *La Cantatrice chauve* (*The Bald Soprano*) heightens the ridiculousness, for there is no soprano in the play, with or without hair. As a theatrical presentation, however—it first went onto the stage at the Théâtre des Noctambules in 1950—it soon becomes tiresome. Making fun of the clichés of the Smiths and the Martins at last becomes itself a cliché. Not everyone can sit through so great a hailstorm of the hackneyed (although readers may enjoy *The Bald Soprano* in the illustrated, album-size Gallimard and Grove Press edition).

Indeed, the first audiences were cold to the play, which closed after a six-weeks' run; audiences were sparse in the little theater. In 1951, Ionesco's second play, *La Leçon* (*The Lesson*), was staged in an even smaller theater, the Théâtre de Poche; spectators were surprised to discover that, in spite of the title, an actual lesson occurred in the play, whose main characters are a professor and a girl student. As in *The Bald Soprano*, Ionesco in *The Lesson* is concerned with semantics, the tyranny of language over thought: in the former play it destroys thought, so that because of their clichés the Smiths and Martins ultimately become interchangeable; in the latter play, language is the instrument of power used by teacher over student. The girl, who has at the first been eager to learn, becomes stupified and takes refuge in a toothache. Then pain spreads through all her body, and the professor, in what is obviously a sexual stroke, stabs her: as staged at the Théâtre de Poche, the girl sat on a chair with her legs spread, and the teacher kept his back to the audience; as he stabbed her, they said "Aaah!" simultaneously, openly suggesting an orgasm. It is the professor's fortieth murder of the day: as the curtain falls, his forty-first victim comes in for her lesson. Ionesco called his play a comic drama; to audiences it conveyed the brutality of the authoritarian.

In *Les Chaises* (1952; *The Chairs*), Ionesco wrote what he called a tragic farce. Because he could find no producer for it, a group of actors arranged to put it on independently in an old hall, the Théâtre Lancry, where it proved to be a failure. Its 1956 revival, however, at the Studio des Champs-Élysées, succeeded. It was played at the Arts Theater in London in 1955 and, with *The Lesson*, at the Royal Court in 1958. At this time the English critic Kenneth Tynan, who had formerly supported Ionesco, found that his work, although "pungent and exciting," was really "a diversion. It is not on the main road." Tynan said the plays avoided social reality. Ionesco answered by asserting that Jean-Paul Sartre, Arthur Miller, John Osborne, and Bertolt Brecht were merely the new boulevard playwrights, with "a left-wing conformism which is just as lamentable as the right-wing sort." What they have to say, people already know from books and speeches; the playwright should instead "offer only a testimony, not a didactic message—a personal, affective testimony of his anguish and the anguish of others or, what is rare, of his happiness." These attacks on other dramatists earned Ionesco some enmity. Philip Toynbee, Orson Welles, and others joined in the controversy, whose issues were never really settled though they helped to indicate how the literature of the absurd can raise exciting questions.

The object of most of this furore, *The Chairs*, is a story of a man and his wife in their nineties, living in a tower on an island and preparing for death. They invite a number of friends and celebrities to hear the old man's testimonial legacy, what he has learned of life, but because he feels incompetent to deliver his statement properly, he has engaged an orator to do so. People begin to arrive, invisible to the audience, and the old couple put out chairs for their guests. Soon the effect of a dense crowd is created. Even the emperor attends. The orator appears, an actor the audience can see and hear. Then the old people go up to jump to their deaths out of an upstairs window into the sea. The orator turns to address the people, but can utter only gibberish. When he tries to write on a blackboard, he produces only a farrago of letters and figures.

In 1953, the year in which seven of Ionesco short pieces (most of them never replayed or published because the manuscripts were lost), appeared at the Huchette, his *Victimes de devoir* (*Victims of Duty*) was staged by Jacques Mauclair at the Théâtre du Quartier Latin. *Victims of Duty*, which Ionesco labeled a pseudo-drama, contains the detective-story element which he believes is an ingredient of all plays. And *Victims of Duty* is a kind of sermon on what theater should be. In the course of the action, a detective asks a man named Choubert whether the previous tenants of his apartment spell their name Mallot or Mallod. Choubert explores the depth of his own unconscious, hence his own past, and enters into fantastically different forms of relationship with his wife. A man who murders the detective finally takes the detective's place as a victim of duty. Ionesco's first three-act play, *Amédée ou comment s'en débarasser* (1954; *Amédée, or How to Get Rid of It*), is the story of a man dragging through the streets a corpse which has long been in his apartment. As Amédée, who is a writer, keeps explaining to the crowds that follow him, he is for socialist realism; what Ionesco thinks of socialist realism is shown when the corpse puffs up and lifts Amédée into the sky.

In an earlier-written play, *Jacques ou la soumission* (*Jack, or the Submission*), produced at the Huchette in 1955, Ionesco presented a comedy of conformism, or at attempts of anticonformism. In a family where everyone is named Jacques (in English, actually James rather than Jack), one of them refuses for a while to utter the standard statement that he likes potatoes fried in lard, but finally he submits and says it. Similarly, when he tries to escape being like everyone else by marrying a girl with three noses, he is offered one with two; upon refusing her, he is offered by her parents another "only daughter," one with three noses. She is not ugly enough, he declares, wanting to be different by having an ugly wife, but the girl finally undermines him sexually: such matters, Ionesco thinks, are at the roots of conformity.

After another series of shorter works, Ionesco in 1959 brought out his second three-act play. The briefer ones, effective in their various ways, include: *Le Tableau* (1955; *The Picture*), *l'Impromptu de l'Alma* (1956; *The Improvisation of Alma*), *Le Nouveau Locataire* (1957; *The New Tenant*), and *l'Avenir est dans les œufs* (1958; *The Future is in the Eggs*). In 1957 a small group, including the Duke and Duchess of Windsor, witnessed a private performance of Ionesco's *Impromptu pour la Duchesse de Windsor* (*Improvisation for the Duchess of Windsor*), a little social comedy. The three-act play of 1959, previously referred to, is *Tueur sans gages* (*Killer Without Payment*, translated as *The Killer*). This is Ionesco's finest work so far.

The idea of the killer without reward, as the original title suggests, brings up the idea of the acte gratuit as used in Gide and other earlier contributors to modern French literature. But the play introduces another theme: the responsibility of the average citizen. That citizen is represented in *The Killer* by Béranger, who rejoices to see a beautiful new quarter of the city. But it is haunted by a murderer. People are afraid of him, but neither the ordinary citizens nor the police seem interested in capturing him. Béranger falls in love with a girl named Dany, who is murdered. Béranger tries to catch the killer, and at last confronts the small, ragged, dirty little man. Béranger tries to appeal to him; he makes a number of indirect statements to see whether the killer has any sense of the social order, of Christianity, of self-preservation, of animals, of the brotherhood of man, of idealism, of reason, even of money. Each time Béranger mentions one of these things, the killer chuckles. He is at the opposite end of twentieth-century literature from Rainer Maria Rilke's poet, who is addressed in "O sage, Dichter, was du tust?— Ich rühme" ("O say, poet, what do you do?—I praise"). Through the interrogation, Rilke's poet is asked how he can bear, how accept, all that is deadly and hideous ("I praise"); how he can call upon what is nameless and anonymous ("I praise"); how he can assume he is right, beneath all costumes and masks ("I praise"); and how both the calm and the violent, the star and the storm, know him for their own ("Because I praise"). How different from Ionesco's gratuitous destroyer, who only giggles unpleasantly at the fundamental questions and, at the last, as Béranger despairs of anything's being done, takes out his knife and draws nearer Béranger, the chuckles still coming as the curtain falls.

Béranger survives, however, at least as a character, for he is in Ionesco's next play, *Rhinocéros*, first staged at

Düsseldorf in 1960, then in Paris by Jean-Louis Barrault, who played Béranger. Laurence Olivier took this rôle in London, in a production directed by Orson Welles, while in New York Eli Wallach played Béranger with Zero Mostel as Jean. The play has been Ionesco's greatest popular success, but it has some obvious drawbacks. True, the symbol of the stampeding rhinoceros is comparatively easy for the average theatergoer to apprehend and, to those seeing it in the theater, the play has great moments of effectiveness, especially when the rhinoceros-herd thunders nearby in the streets, and the various actors stop speaking, freeze their faces, and turn their eyes in terror. But gradually the characters in the play succumb to the prevalent, highly contagious rhinoceros fever, which is of course Ionesco's old enemy, conformism. He had watched people go stamping and shouting into the Nazi movement of the 1930's, and he recalled a description of a Nuremberg crowd by the Swiss writer, Denis de Rougement, at a moment when Hitler arrived: as an anti-Nazi, de Rougement watched the frenzy of the crowd with astonishment, then gradually felt himself being drawn in, toward participation, and he had to fight against his impulses with his whole being. In *Rhinocéros*, Béranger watches his girl, Daisy, and his friend, Jean, drawn toward rhinoceros-hood, slowly giving way to the shaking of the legs and, in the case of Jean, to the bellowing (at which Zero Mostel was frighteningly good in the Broadway version). Béranger alone fights against the disease, even when he feels it stirring in his limbs. For a moment he even thinks that, in not becoming a rhinoceros, he is a monster, but then he decides to fight against the entire world and looks for his gun: "I'm the last man, I'll fight it out to the bitter end. I'm not giving up!"

This last seems weak in the theater, as it does in reading: it is too obvious an assertion, however much Ionesco was praised for taking a stand, at last, that seemed positive. He expressed regret because the play was taken as a comedy in New York and elsewhere, for to him it is a tragedy, though at the same time a farce. He wondered how many people really understand the tragedy of "massification."

As noted earlier, the absurd is limited. Sitting in the theater, one becomes weary of the clocks that strike seventeen. Even when Ionesco becomes engaged and struggles against the absurd, as in *Rhinocéros*, he doesn't deepen or extend the possibilities of his created world; he merely beats against its limitations.

4 *Further Dramatists of the Absurd: Adamov and Arrabal*

Arthur Adamov (born 1908) and Fernando Arrabal (born 1932) are two other playwrights who work within the milieu of the absurd. Adamov, an Armenian born in Russia, spent most of his early life in Switzerland, moving to Paris at sixteen to become part of the surréaliste group. For several years before and during the Second World War, he worked on an existentialiste-like self-revelation, *l'Aveu* (1946; *The Confession*). It was after completing this that he turned to the theater. He has said that his first play, the third to be produced—*La Parodie* (1952; *The Parody*)—was inspired by a street scene: two girls who bumped into a blind beggar were singing a song about closing one's eyes, and oh! it was wonderful ("J'ai fermé les yeux, c'était merveilleux"). The irony struck Adamov, who had been reading August Strindberg and was particularly moved by *A Dream Play*. In *The Parody*, a girl is loved by two men who don't know how to approach her properly, with futility as the result. One of the mocking features of this piece is a clock without hands.

Before *The Parody* was produced at the Lancry by Roger Blin, two other plays by Adamov had appeared in Paris little theaters: *l'Invasion* (1950) and *La Grande et la Petite Manœuvre* (1950; *The Large and the Small Maneuver*). *The Invasion* is virtually a theater-of-the-absurd parody on themes familiar to Henry James, who in *The Aspern Papers* wrote of the problems of dealing with an author's manuscripts after his death, and who in *The Figure in the Carpet* dealt with the subject of what a writer really meant, showing that others very rarely knew. In *The Invasion*, Pierre gets hold of the papers left by his late brother-in-law, a famous writer, and as he tries to put them in order he can't decipher them. Pierre's death leaves the problem up in the air—or on paper.

The Large and Small Maneuver takes place in a police state in which the revolutionary leader proves to be no more effective in his life-activity than the helpless character without arms and legs who is at another level the victim of the dictatorship: this mutilé becomes increasingly more crippled as the play goes on, just as the revolutionary leader becomes progressively more helpless.

Adamov's next two plays were first produced together at Lyon in 1953. *Le Sens de la marche* (*The Direction of the March*) is the story of a young man, Henri, haunted by his father, whom he sees in all guises of authority, everywhere he goes. When he returns to the home of his dead father, he finds that the latter's former masseur has taken over domination of the household as well as Henri's sister. Henri murders him. *Le Professeur Taranne*, the idea of which came to Adamov in a dream, about himself, concerns the troubles of a highly respectable professional man accused of indecent exposure, which he furiously denies. But Adamov seems to be proving that a man can be a creative and valuable member of the community at the same time he is something else.

With *Tous contre tous* (1953; *Everyone Against Everyone*), Adamov returned to the police-state setting. Adamov said, "I wanted to convey my own fright to others." In this play, there is an influx of refugees from abroad, all identified easily because they limp; the symbolism is readily apparent. These refugees are far from perfect: they seize power and hold it for a while, only to lose it again. The keynote of the play is sounded by the girl Noémi, who says, "One can't live in constant fear, it's impossible, it cries out for vengeance at the last." Adamov created a play more deeply in the spirit of the absurd in

Le Ping-pong (1951), in which a pinball machine that fascinates two young men becomes a monster dominating the action. They abandon their potential careers in art and medicine to take up the manufacture of pinball machines, and the concept of these machines—of the machine itself—controls their lives. They are last seen as old men playing ping-pong, with one of them dropping dead. After Adamov had achieved this masterpiece of the absurd, he turned to another kind of writing in *Paolo Paoli* (1957), which really belongs to the epic theater of Bertolt Brecht.

Paolo Paoli is a panoramic play of the years 1900–14, dealing with the background events leading up to the first war. The play has only a small group of characters, but the effect of massed events is conveyed by occasional flashing onto a screen of the headlines of the period, while the popular songs of different years are played. In the story, Paoli is a man who collects rare butterflies; a friend of his imports ostrich feathers. The theater of the absurd is still present, however, particularly in the importance given to butterflies and ostrich feathers in world trade. The influence of religion and politics is also shown, for the play is intricate; indeed, as the war draws near, politics become the principal theme, and the rôle of economics—trade—is stressed. In *Le Printemps '71* (1960; *Spring '71*), Adamov again attempts social panorama, this time in a play dealing with Paris at the time of the Commune. But even in this realistic projection of history, Adamov couldn't altogether do without some of the mechanics of the absurd, for between the principal episodes he introduced sequences in which puppets made fun of the principal personages and events of the time.

Adamov's post-absurd plays have disappointed many of his earlier admirers. Throughout his work there has generally been a lack of human feeling, partly because the author is always the victim of ideas and doctrines: he sometimes seems like Pierre in *The Invasion*, trying to decipher meaning from heaps of manuscripts. If the plays of Adamov do not hold together in dramatic cohesion,

with the interrelationship of people and ideas imple-
mented, he has nevertheless provided some fine theatrical
moments, as in the terror conveyed in parts of his dramas
about dictators.

Fernando Arrabal, from what was formerly Spanish
Morocco, studied law in Madrid, but in 1954, when he
was twenty-two, he moved to France and has written in
French. The characters in his plays are exceptionally
simple, naïve types who find themselves in the world of
the absurd. In *Pique-nique en campagne* (1958; *Picnic on
the Battlefield*), for example, a young soldier whose
parents have come to visit him at the front is having a
picnic with them behind the lines, and they even invite
an enemy soldier he has captured; but eventually all these
innocents are wiped out by machine-gun fire. Similar
occurrences mark Arrabal's other plays, of which the two-
act drama, *Le Cimitière des voitures* (1958; *The Graveyard of Automobiles*) penetrates farthest into the absurd.
In the junkland of rotting old cars, a group of people live
ceremoniously, including a thirty-three-year-old trumpet
player named Emanou who is, in the symbolism of the
play, Emmanuel, or the Christ. He is betrayed to the
police by a kiss, and after he has been strenuously beaten,
he is taken away to his death, crucified on the handle-bars
of a bicycle, as life resumes in the raggle-taggle setting.
Emanou, who is, emblematically, the son of a carpenter,
has tried to pursue simple goodness in an absurd world.

Arrabal, in addition to his contributions to the literature of the absurd, has shown an interest in theatrical
abstraction, as in his *Orchestration théâtral* (1959). This
play without words takes place in a landscape reminiscent
of Paul Klee inhabited by the mobiles of Alexander
Calder. Despite the inclusion of dancers, the public didn't
respond to this attempt to give abstract art a new
dimension.

5 The Mud and Ashcan World
of Samuel Beckett

Samuel Beckett's career is in some ways incredible, for he is an obscurantist whose plays fill theaters and whose novels move well in the bookstores. In the United States, more than a quarter-million volumes of his works have been sold. But Beckett may not be too obscurantist after all: his success may come from his discovery and projection of obscurantist elements in the lives of everyone today. The absurd elements, too.

Beckett's recent life emphasizes the elements of mystery and isolation found in his work. Since the Second World War, in which he saw noncombatant service, he has lived in France as a virtual recluse. He is an Irishman who has often written in French.

Born in a Protestant family in Dublin in 1906, Beckett attended Portora Royal School at Enniskillen, where he was a popular athlete, playing both cricket and Rugger. He studied French and Italian at Trinity College, Dublin, from which he received his B.A. in 1927. As an exchange lecteur for two years at the École normale supérieure in Paris, he knew Jean-Paul Sartre. After going back to Dublin for his M.A. in 1931, Beckett traveled on the Continent. The death of his father in 1933 made him, in a modest way, financially independent, and finally, in 1937, he settled in Paris. By this time he had published four books, two of them volumes of poetry, as well as various articles and stories. One of his first pieces to appear in print was his essay on the influence of Vico, Dante, and Bruno on Joyce's *Finnegans Wake*, which was at that time called *Work in Progress*: Beckett's article first appeared in *transition* in June, 1929 and, later that year, as one of the contributions to the volume *An Exagmination of James Joyce*.

It was in the next year that Beckett's first book came out, a four-page poem with extensive notes, entitled *Whoroscope*. Nancy Cunard first published it as a product of The Hours Press, which had conducted a contest for a poem about time, which *Whoroscope* won (it has since been reprinted in Beckett's *Poems in English* in 1961). *Whoroscope*, not only because of its notes, but because of its form, the dramatic monologue, suggests the early poetry of T. S. Eliot, but it also has affinities with the universal dream Joyce was projecting in *Work in Progress*. Further, *Whoroscope* indicates Beckett's interest in Descartes, who in the poem is dealing with an egg that is both symbolic (universal birth) and part of an omelette.

Beckett in 1931 brought out a small book on Proust, witty and wordy, and in 1934 a collection of ten stories, *More Pricks Than Kicks*. In 1938 his first novel, *Murphy*, was published in London (as the earlier book of fiction had been), and it quietly sank into an oblivion that was not to prove permanent. Murphy is one of Beckett's unhappy city-men, surrounded by London (edge of Chelsea) grotesque types and presented in a language full of puns and Cartesian allusions, reflecting Descartes's mathematical logic of "I think, therefore I am." It is Murphy's fate to be destroyed by fire, foretelling the fate of what was left of the first edition of the book (most of it), which was destroyed by flames during a wartime air raid on London. As for Murphy in the story, his ashes, brought back to Dublin, are scattered on the floor of a pub during a brawl, rather than, as he had wished, being flushed down the toilet at the Abbey Theater.

While living in Paris, Beckett was often the escort of Joyce's odd, intense, attractive daughter Lucia, who was later put into an asylum. She fell violently in love with Beckett, who couldn't reciprocate the affection. Perhaps because of this, Beckett moved to London for a while, living in Chelsea. About three years before the war, a man came up to Beckett in a Paris street and suddenly stabbed him, perforating his lung. Joyce telephoned to doctors in London, but the wound doesn't seem to have been too serious after all, and before long Beckett was released from the hospital. He visited the prison where the man who had stabbed him was confined. Beckett asked the man why he had attacked him, and the man gave a reply that seems to come out of a Beckett story or play: "I don't know."

Between *Murphy* in 1938 and the appearance of some poems, prose, and prose poems in French in 1946, there is a hiatus in Beckett's bibliography, accounted for partly by his wartime activities, and partly by his delay in publishing the novel, *Watt*, which he wrote at this time; at the urging of friends, he finally brought it out, via the Olympia Press, in 1953. He had been in Ireland when the war started and had at once returned to France, saying that he "preferred France in war to Ireland in peace." In Paris he engaged in activities against the Nazis until the arrest of Alfred Péron, who had worked with him on parts of the translation of Joyce's *Work in Progress*. Beckett disappeared from Paris shortly before the Nazis pounded into his own apartment. He went to Vaucleuse, in the unoccupied zone, and it was there he wrote *Watt*. Beckett went back to Ireland for a while, returning to France in 1945 as a Red Cross storekeeper and interpreter. He was under heavy fire at St. Lô, and for a while had to lie flat in a graveyard in order to avoid being hit by exploding shells. His friend Perón, who had been deported to Germany, died in a concentration camp there in 1945.

By the end of the war Beckett had begun to write in French, sometimes translating his works into English. In 1947 he rewrote the English version of *Murphy*, putting it into French (its English version has reappeared in the appropriate countries). In 1951 and 1953 he brought out the three volumes known as his trilogy, the *Molloy-Malone Dies-The Unnamable* books, which will be discussed after *Watt*. In that novel, or antinovel, a rather repellent man named Watt, who continually blows his nose in toilet paper, is a candidate for an asylum, though in the interim he acts as a servant (or nonservant) in the pseudo-Irish farmhouse of a Mr. Knott. A searcher after reality and of the offstage Mr. Knott, Watt spends part of his time inventing a comic language. Mr. Knott always keeps dogs to eat the left over food from his table; when there isn't enough they die of starvation, and when there is too much they die of overeating. As his mysteriously appointed time is mysteriously up, Watt goes on the journey whose end finds him in a garden, apparently of an asylum. A haggard clown, who in smiling seems to be sucking his teeth, Watt is another of Beckett's low-life masks of Everyman, this one a Watt-ness in grotesque search of a Knott-ness, questing in terms that lampoon the very processes of logic.

The previously mentioned trilogy was written in French and translated by Beckett (sometimes in collaboration) into English: *Molloy* (1951), *Malone meurt* (1951; *Malone Dies*), and *l'Innomable* (1953; *The Unnamable*). Critics have found in these books the Cartesian skepticism; in them and in Beckett's other work a shift from metaphysics (the nature of being) to epistemology (the nature of knowledge); or a relationship between man as machine and man as user of machine (as in the case of Molloy's bicycle); or a Dantean tripartite afterworld of hell, purgatory, and heaven; or a "zero depth" of writing; or the extreme mythological projection of the Doppelgänger; or nonnaming of the unnamable and nonsaying of the unsayable; or a picture of total disintegration; or inventors inventing themselves—and so on. Molloy is a partially crippled man on a bicycle, looking for his lost home town and his dying mother, and in turn being sought by Moran, on another bicycle, who doesn't find him but becomes crippled like him and passes from his own state of moralism to Molloy's amoralism. Malone, dying in a room he can't place geographically, is able at least to write stories—puzzling and absurd—on his deathbed. In the third volume, the Unnamable, who is also unplaceable—without place and deaf, dumb, and mostly blind—can only float through a half-realized existence, under the spell of deceptive identities. All three books are monologues: in the first there are two, Molloy's and Moran's, in the second only Malone's, and in the third only that of the Unnamable, which isn't even quite a monologue. These books are the extreme of both antiliterature and the absurd. Much has been made over the recurrence of m's in the names and titles.

In 1949, *transition* printed several conversations between Beckett and the historian of Byzantine art, Georges Duthuit, in the course of which Beckett proposed a theory of artistic nihilism and, when Duthuit asked him whether he realized that what he was suggesting was absurd, Beckett said that he did. His work has been from the first absurd. The Cartesian aspects of it are perhaps most fully developed in the monologues of the trilogy, where the characters exist only because they think, and where they think only about themselves, with the external world growing increasingly dimmer. There is also the word-world of Joyce, which Beckett transfers from language to language. And he always seems to be in Kafka's land of unattainable goals (Molloy's not finding his town and his dying mother) and of half-understood or half-expressed statements (Moran's not being told exactly whom he is to look for, yet halfway knowing as he goes on his futile quest). Yet, for all his kinship with these concepts, men, and influences, Beckett's vision seems distinctly his own. The rhythm of his thought and utterance is highly individualistic.

Beckett, besides writing for the theater, continued to turn out short fiction and poetry, as well as such productions as *Comment c'est* (1961; *How It Is*), which is an extremely antinovel type of "novel." Taking up nearly one hundred and forty pages in Beckett's English translation, the book is written in unpunctuated paragraphs, usually short. The setting is a kind of elemental mud, in which naked man is crawling with a sack which contains a few precious cans of different kinds of fish; he also has a can opener. Wriggling through the mud, which may be manure as easily as mud, the protagonist encounters another figure slithering along, face down: this is Pim, who can be made to talk by the can opener's prodding him in the buttocks, and who can be silenced by having his face jammed down into the mud. The narrator enjoys

the time with Pim, but according to the laws of an
unexplained necessity, he must crawl on and leave Pim,
who also has a sack. So:

> alone in the mud yes the dark yes sure yes panting yes
> someone hears me no no one hears me no murmuring some-
> times yes when the panting stops yes not at other times no
> in the mud yes to the mud yes my voice yes not another's
> no mine alone yes sure yes when the panting stops yes on
> and off yes a few words yes a few scraps yes that no one
> hears no but less and less no answer LESS AND LESS yes

> so things may change no answer and no answer I may choke
> no answer sink no answer sully the mud no more no answer
> the dark no answer trouble the peace no more answer the
> silence no answer die no answer DIE screams I MAY DIE
> screams I SHALL DIE screams good

> good good end at last of part three and that's how it was
> end of quotation after Pim how it is

—and so ends the third, post-Pim part of this "novel,"
whose first two parts might be called pre-Pim and Pimself.
The poetic quality of the book will have conveyed itself to
the reader even through these short closing extracts; and if
anyone says this seems incoherent, let him reflect whether
it is any more incoherent than life is today in the noisy
and glittering world. The symbols are not difficult to
speculate about: the sack may be the womb as well as the
tomb (and sackcloth may have a special suggestion); the
fish foods provide a Christian symbol, and even Christian
symbols may occur amid the essential nihilism; the
preciously guarded can opener may be the emblem of
man's mechanical effort, or the nails of Christ, or both.
There are also a cord, a comb and, above all (really
beneath all, or pervading all), the primeval slime in which
Everyman (as well as another Everyman, Beckett's usual
Doppelgänger) still pushes his way along—toward what?

Beckett's first public success came with his play *En
attendant Godot* (*Waiting for Godot*), which quite
absurdly made him a popular author. It was first produced
in Paris in 1953, in London in 1955, and in New York in

1956. Reviewing the original French production, at the little avant-garde Théâtre de Babylone, Jean Anouilh wrote that the play was "a performance of Pascal's *Pensées* as acted by the Fratinelli clowns." And indeed, the two leading characters, Vladimir (Didi) and Estragon (Gogo) were made up, in that original production by Roger Blin, as they have usually been in subsequent presentations in other countries, like clowns: they suggest not only the Fratintellis but the bums of the old Mack Sennett comedies. And, in addition to Commedia dell' arte figures, they also evoke the much-abused, seri-comic tramp that Chaplin played when he long ago demonstrated that, with all the richness of the earth and the opulence that human beings have taken from it, such elements as poverty, vagabondage, and an underworld are absurd. But Didi and Gogo represent more than mere physical poverty: they are also modern man's spiritual penury.

These two tramps wait for a couple of days by a gallows-like tree for a Godot who doesn't appear. A boy, however, comes to notify Didi and Gogo that Godot isn't going to arrive. They have meanwhile watched the antics of Pozzo and Lucky, master and slave, rope-bound to one another in a ridiculous manner: at one point Lucky, who carries a weighted suitcase he refuses to put down, makes a long, incoherent, pun-strewn, *Finnegans Wake*-like speech that comes to an end only when Didi seizes Lucky's hat, which is in effect his thinking cap. Later, Pozzo goes blind though he pretends not to be; the tree has put forth a few leaves, the only actual "progress" of anything in the story, mocking Vladimir and Estragon, who early in the play and then toward the end consider suicide but finally refrain from attempting it largely because they can't figure how to hang themselves from the tree without a rope. The play closes with Didi asking, "Alors? On y va?" ("Well? Shall we go?") and Gogo replying, "Allons-y" ("Yes, let's go").

The play was so successful at the Babylone that, after four hundred performances, it moved to the Hébertot.

Similarly, in London it went from the Arts Theater to the Criterion after "a small number of textual deletions were made to satisfy the Lord Chamberlain." Its success in these cities and elsewhere is astounding because, despite whatever William Saroyan and others may have said, *Godot* is a formless play. Usually, in the theater we expect a beginning-middle-end development because that is the shape of a story, the shape of what the mind expects. Leave out an element in your tale, and someone will ask, "But what of—?" or "What happened next?" On the other hand, someone who is reading a story may, if bored, skip the uninteresting parts; the time element is unimportant. But someone listening to a tale, or watching a play, is trapped: the boredom can devour him, as in Eugene O'Neill's *Long Day's Journey Into Night* or in Edward Albee's *Who's Afraid of Virginia Woolf?*, whose repetitive scenes can become physically unbearable to someone pinned down in the theater. Reading on one's own is an activity that doesn't depend upon consecutive time, as watching a dramatic performance does. *Godot*, it is true, has a certain amount of suspense because the audience wonders whether or not Godot will actually appear—and yet there are long stretches of the play which do not further what we would ordinarily mean by the action. Normally, such failing to reach the dramatic point creates boredom in the audience, yet the international success of *Godot* suggests that Beckett's narrative-rather-dramatic mode of presentation either doesn't produce ennui or that the popularity of the play may be attributed almost entirely to vogue, a quite likely possibility. Whatever the cause, the play really set a style, so that theater audiences, instead of looking for the types of play produced yesterday —and this doesn't at all refer to the so-called well-made play—are now often confronted with novels which are merely acted out. For essentially that is what such plays as *Waiting for Godot* are. To say this is not to detract from Beckett's play, which is notable for the differences in characterization between Estragon and Vladimir, the effective symbolic leashing together of Pozzo and Lucky, the spurts of comedy, the sense of mystery generated by the unseen, unknown Godot, and by the play's significant revelation of the absurdity of much human activity.

The producer of *Godot*, Roger Blin, also staged *Fin de partie* (1957; *Endgame*) at the Studio des Champs-Élysées. The title of this one-act play is taken from a chess term signifying the third and last part of the match. The action takes place—if it can really be said to take place—on a bare stage, in grey light, with two ashcans at one side. The blind and invalid Hamm, in a wheelchair, is tended—or not tended—by the malignantly comic Clov. Hamm's parents, Nagg and Nell, who have lost their legs in an accient, occasionally raise the lids of the ashcans to speak. Nell dies during the play, and perhaps Hamm dies at the end of it, when he puts back over his face the bloody handkerchief that had been covering it when the curtain went up. There are suggestions, from some of the biblical echoes in the language, that Hamm is the crucified Christ, and because of the chess-game symbolism (suggesting Ferdinand and Miranda) the play has been compared to Shakespeare's *The Tempest*, whose famous line, "Our revels now are ended," is quoted in the English version. But Christ's death meant hope, and Prospero, after drowning his book, was taking his daughter back to live in the world: *Endgame* is a play about the death of hope, and perhaps about the death of the world itself. All this is conveyed with tremendous dramatic effectiveness, with the dire hopelessness emphasized by such statements as Hamm's "You're on earth, and there's no cure for that!"

In the London production of 1958, the despair was partly mitigated by another one-act play of Beckett's which appeared with *Endgame*, one he wrote in English: *Krapp's Last Tape*. Brief as it is, this is one of Beckett's finest theatrical efforts, and even though it has only one character it gives an impression of fullness. Krapp is one of Beckett's untidy old men, except that he has not been altogether untidy in keeping records of his past: he has recorded his life on a series of tapes, some of which he plays back during the performance. Krapp, shuffling and snuffling, takes out the spools of tape, talking to himself, drawing out the word spool at great length and with great relish. As he plays the spools, his past—love affairs, the time his mother was dying—blooms out in his shabby quarters. Krapp munches bananas that he keeps taking out of his pocket, sucks at a liquor bottle, thinks of his book which had sold seventeen copies, and laughs and broods over his former self. ("What's a year now? The sour cud and the iron stool.") At sixty-nine, Krapp hears his thirty-nine-year-old self say, "Perhaps my best years are gone. When there was a chance of happiness. But I wouldn't want them back. Not with the fire in me now. No, I wouldn't want them back." Krapp stares motionless before him as the tape runs on in silence and the curtain slowly comes down on this haunting exploration of the self.

There is a wry comedy in the situation, and also sadness, but not the despair of *Endgame*: rather, *Krapp's Last Tape* is for the most part a lament for the passing of time, and it is this, with change inevitably leading to decay, that produces the sorrow of the world. There is in addition some sterner philosophy, an attempt to realize the essence of the self, partly in Cartesian terms; in that only the present, thinking self (thinking however dimly) is actual, and the past self seems unreal, existing outside the subjective ranges of the consciousness.

There is also, in *Krapp's Last Tape*, a suggestion of the discussions of the awareness of the self in David Hume's *Treatise on Human Nature*: "For my part, when I enter most intimately into what I call *myself* I always stumble on some particular perception or other, of heat or cold, light or shade, love or hatred, pain or pleasure. I can never catch *myself* at any time without a perception, and can never observe anything but the perception. . . . The mind is a kind of theater where several perceptions successively make their appearance, pass, and re-pass, glide away and mingle in an infinite variety of postures and situations. There is no proper *simplicity* in it at any one time, nor *identity* in different, whatever natural propension we may have to imagine that simplicity and identity. The comparison of the theater must not mislead us. They are successive perceptions only that constitute the mind; nor have we the most distant notion of the place where these scenes are represented, or of the materials of which it is composed." Further, *Krapp's Last Tape* examines time itself, partly (as if to contradict the Cartesianism) in terms resembling T. S. Eliot's statements in "Burnt Norton," from *Four Quartets*:

> If all time is eternally present,
> All time is unredeemable.
>
> . . . .
>
> What might have been and what has been
> Point to one end, which is always present.

Beckett also wrote some radio plays, including *All That Fall* (1957) and *Embers* (1960), presented on BBC's Third Programme, *Acte sans paroles I* (*Act Without Words I*) and *Acte sans paroles II* (*Act Without Words II*), which he translated from the French. In 1964 Beckett made his first trip to the United States, to supervise the production of a moving picture made from his work by Evergreen Films, starring Buster Keaton. Two of Beckett's later important plays were written in English: *Happy Days* (1961) and *Play* (1963). In *Happy Days*, a hideously ironic title, the curtain goes up on a woman named Winnie who is breezily cheerful although buried up to her breast in earth. She prays, she brushes her teeth, she chatters in clichés, she quotes or misquotes the poets, she invents people, and although she has greeted the day as "another happy day," she yearns for sleep. Her husband, Willie, with whom she has been trying to communicate, at last crawls along and gets into the mound where Winnie is buried, as she intones, "This is a happy day. This will have been another happy day."

By this time, students of Beckett may well wonder where the explorer of the absurd can go next: in which ashcan or mound will be embed his people? The writer of tragedy has no such problem, for tragedy can deal intensively with love, ambition, jealousy, and other themes, while the writer of comedy can treat, in reverse, these and other topics; and the ironist can go in the direction of either comedy or tragedy. But the writer of the absurd is at a continual dead end: we can wait only so long for Godot. When *Happy Days* opened in New York, Robert Brustein, one of the finest drama critics in the world, noted that Beckett was plainly in a dilemma, that "he has a single, all-encompassing vision of existence which leads him to seek not new themes but new metaphors with which to dramatize the same theme. . . . It remains to be seen whether Beckett will remain in the ditch, or will develop in an entirely new direction. But whatever the future holds, his place in the drama is secure. In a world of the tenth-rate, even the minor work of this man is like an orient pearl."

Certainly Beckett has made important contributions to both English and French literature, and in the literature of the absurd he is a giant.

And in writing so much of his work in the language of his adopted country, as well as reflecting much of its spirit as this has manifested itself in terms of modernism, Beckett has joined with other foreign-born writers to infuse new blood into modern French writing. In so doing, these authors have increased the richness and variety of modern French literature and have helped to make it, in the principal genres, the outstanding literature of Continental Europe in this century.

INDEX

FRANCE, a country which accords status to authors, has produced many influential modern writers. This introduction to recent French literature provides not only interesting reading but also useful critical analysis of modern French poetry, fiction, and drama. As the title indicates, *Twentieth-Century French Literature since World War II* begins with postwar writing and carries up to the early 1960's. Thus it covers relatively current work, varying from traditional to absurd; all types are considered here.

Harry T. Moore has woven an interesting account of the literature of the postwar period by giving biographical, social, and political backgrounds, and he freely uses extracts for concrete illustration. Publication dates, names of theaters and actors, and translations of titles are given in the text so that there is no necessity for turning to a note or bibliography section for these details.

The first chapter is devoted to postwar poetry, although mention is made of the prewar and wartime writings of such poets as Ponge, Michaux, Prévert, and Char. The philosophical work of Bonnefoy is discussed as well as the writings of several other younger poets. Drama flourished after the Second World War, and the chapter on the theater simultaneously examines playwriting and producing, often noting the leading actors and theaters associated with the postwar renascence of French drama. Topics which were taboo during the war could now be brought to the stage, and Salacrou wrote of the résistance and German occupation. Anouilh, Montherlant, Francois Mauriac, Bernanos, Green, and many others are discussed, and the wide range of drama from traditional to existentialiste is nicely illustrated.

Existentialisme, which began before the Second World War and is discussed in a companion volume by Mr. Moore [*French Literature to World War II*], is elaborated further in the longest chapter of the present book. The doctrine is reviewed, and the later careers of Jean-Paul Sartre and Albert Camus as well as Simone de Beauvoir are thoroughly con-

[Continued on back]